Growing up in Garfield

Jim Connelly

Other Books by Jim Connelly

Tom and Anna on the Trail: the Case of the Missing Schoolgirl (2014)

Tom and Anna in Danger: the Case of the Disappearing Dogs (2014)

Tom and Anna take a Chance: the Case of the Bungling Bird Bandits (2015)

My Folk: Four Hundred Years of Hazards, Tooths, and Connellys (2015)

Mountain Boy (2016)

Talk of the Town: Warragul/Drouin (2017)

Talk of the Town (2): Warragul/Drouin (2018)

Pickled Pieces and Rollicking Rhymes (2019)

Wild Beauty (2019)

Round and About in Gippsland (2020)

Father Jeremy (2020)

Growing up in Garfield

Jim Connelly

Copyright

Copyright Jim Connelly 2021

Paperback ISBN 978-0-6486658-3-0

All rights reserved

No part of this publication may be reproduced or

transmitted in any form or by any means, electronic or

mechanical, including photocopying, recording, or any

information storage system, without prior

permission in writing of the copyright owner.

A CIP catalogue record for this book is available from the

National Library of Australia

First published in Australia 2021 by

James Timothy Connelly

12 Craig Street,

Warragul, Victoria, 3820

AUSTRALIA

ajcon@dcsi.net.au

For my parents and Tessy and Angela, in fond memory, and for Noel

Cover design by Craig Braithwaite, *Aussiepics*

Foreword

Woody Allen once said the one regret in his life was that he was not someone else. We've all felt that way at times. Alas! The rules don't allow it. All we can do is stick with who we are, and make the best of it.

That's the sentiment behind this work. Not only have I given up on trying to be someone else, I've come to the point where I don't hide my light under the nearest bushel. So here I am offering myself – at least my young self - for your critical and psychological examination.

But it's not all about me. It's about the life and times that shaped me. So if you tire of hearing about me, just read the other parts.

Please be kind in your judgments, but if you do find anything detrimental to my character, let me know and I'll sue the author for defamation.

Jim Connelly, September, 2021

Growing up in Garfield

Chapter 1

I grew up in Garfield.

Garfield is a name to be proud of. There are Garfields in Minnesota, New Jersey, Georgia, Kansas, and Washington State. In Wisconsin there are three Garfields. Linda Bove, the deaf Librarian in Sesame Street, came from Garfield, New Jersey.

There is a Mount Garfield in New Zealand, but it is in the middle of nowhere.

Garfield, Victoria, Australia, the Garfield I grew up in, is really somewhere, as you will hear.

There is a cat Garfield - a fat cat who eats lasagne. There are sixty-two Garfield cat books.

There is no book about Garfield, Victoria, Australia, until this one.

Before Garfield was named Garfield, it was known as Cannibal Creek. I've heard it said many times that Garfield is not a particularly pretty name, but it's much better than Cannibal Creek. Cannibal Creek runs four or five kilometres north of where Garfield is now. But when a railway was built through the region, the timber that used to be carted to Melbourne by bullock wagon was loaded on to the new train trucks instead. So the town moved to the railway line, but kept the old name – Cannibal Creek Siding.

That is until the Republican President of faraway United States, James Abram Garfield, was shot by Charles Guiteau. Guiteau was a lawyer. Normally, people take their grievances to a lawyer. In this case the lawyer took his grievances to the President. President Garfield's death was very unfortunate. Not because he was a Republican, but because he was a very good President. In his honour there is a statue of him in front of the Congress building in Washington, DC. I have a photo of him and me standing there together. But more importantly, a bevy of Garfields sprang up across the globe. Mostly in the United States, as we've seen, but also in Gippsland, Victoria, Australia.

This outburst of affection in Australia for a deceased American President is an honourable thing, but is not easy to understand. There is no record of engagement with the United States amongst the residents of the former Cannibal Creek Siding. The other thing is that the name change to Garfield didn't happen until 1887, six years after President Garfield's death. Perhaps the enthusiasm for the American relationship amongst the local people was not as strong as one might imagine.

To my regret, I have to confess I was not actually born in Garfield itself, but nearby, in Melbourne. My mother, fearing that there might be some risk in having this fourth child, went off to the Women's Hospital to bear me. She was staying in Williamstown with my Aunty Vivien beforehand, and took the train into the city for the birth. Aunty Vivien watched the train pull out of the station, my mother's haggard face carrying all the marks of impending doom. All went well, however, and a telegram was sent off to my father, "Son born Saturday night. Both well". This has caused me some grief over the years, as I was actually born early on Sunday morning. So I am blithe and bonny and good and gay as the nursery rhyme says, and do not have to work hard for my living as Saturday children have to do. As events have turned out, perhaps I should have been born on Saturday night after all. This birth occurred on July the thirtieth, 1933, which was a time when Melbourne and the world were in the pit of the Great Depression. The story goes that although I was healthy to a degree – weighing ten pounds - the babies in all the wards around were pitifully ill and malnourished, their sad cries echoing through the halls of the hospital.

There are two other absorbing facts about my birth. The first is that I was born with a caul over my face. A caul is a membrane that can cover the head parts of a baby, and is immediately removed by the doctor or midwife. This happens in fewer than one in 80,000 births, which makes me something of a prodigy. Lord Byron, George Formby, and Liberace were all born with a caul. And me. It's always been believed that a caul-bearer would never drown. That has been proved correct in my own case, though I still step carefully when cleaning the pool.

The other thing is that I can remember being born. I have been telling people this all my life, but meet only looks of silent disbelief. There are two ways of knowing something, I say. One is to know it objectively and the other is to know it instinctively. This memory of mine belongs in the second category, but is none the less true. Ask Professors of Sociology, who rely on this claim entirely to make a living. Having proved my case, I can now describe my memory of birth as a sensation of consistent, furry, inevitable rollingness, like a ball rolling across a table-top, gathering pace, and nothing, nothing at all, can stop it, and accompanied by a low hum of sound, rather like a muffled drum roll, unlike any other experience known to humankind. There! Take it or leave it!

To begin our Garfield experience, we lived for a couple of years in a rented house on the Swamp, in Brownbill Road, off the Thirteen Mile Road. The house was owned by a Mrs Dickson or Dixon. The Koo Wee Rup Swamp is a vast tract of land that was once unusable and uninhabitable, but which was drained a hundred years ago, and now makes up some of the State's best agricultural land. Just before we arrived there from Pearcedale, the great 1934 flood occurred. Perhaps that's why the house was available!

By the time I came to the age of remembering, we were living in another rented house we called, 'Webb's'. I presume Mr Webb was the owner. He must have been an absentee landlord for we never saw him. This house was a small timber building at the eastern end of Archer Road in

Garfield. In our time, however, the road was called Slaughterhouse Road. To get into town, we walked about half a mile to the main road, Government Road, now known as Garfield Road. Then it was another quarter of a mile down the steep Garfield Hill to the town. The slaughter yard paddocks were across the road from our place. One of our great delights was to find jawbones from slaughtered sheep, which made perfect hand-guns, the more teeth remaining, the finer the weapon. The dirt road was ideal for marbles. My mother once said that the first sign she ever saw that I had my own marbles was that I quickly learnt how to play the game by watching the others. We called marbles 'alleys' with the stress on the first syllable.

My sisters and brother were already going to school at this time, while I was resting at home. There were six of us. Daddy and Mummy, Tessy and Angela, Noel and Jim. That list is to be read in the same cadence as I would recite it in my prayers each night. 'God bless Daddy and Mummy …' and the rest. From here onward, my parents will be referred to in more adult terms. Dad was William Francis Connelly and Mum was Joyce Winifred Connelly, nee Hazard. Mum always referred to Dad as 'Will', though people outside the family like Mr Pratt called him 'Bill'. As for Dad, he never called Mum by name ever. They married in 1924 when Dad was thirty-two and Mum was twenty-three. Mum had come out from England after the First World War, when she was twenty-one. She was from a family of seven children. They belonged to the Established Church and lived in a grand house and went to good schools. The children had huge fun together, doing imaginative things, writing and acting and playing in the river meadows. However the War put an end to that. Her father lost his money; her favourite brother was killed in France; the family was broken up. Mum fled to Australia. With Dad, it was quite the opposite. He was third-generation Australian of Irish Catholic descent, and came from a struggling rural background at Learmonth near Ballarat. His parents died when he was in his mid-teens. He served on the Western Front, was captured at Bullecourt, and spent the last eighteen months of the War in a German prison camp.

I don't remember Dad being there very much in the early days, and I think that must have been because he was away digging potatoes at Neerim or Neerim South or perhaps other places. Before we came to Garfield, Dad had his own place at Pearcedale, but that had proved a failure and he was now a day labourer. He carried the scars of that failure for all time. My mother was very much there. She it was who rescued me from a snake nicely curled up in the front garden and which I, in my infant way, had mistaken for a lizard. Once my mother and father had a bitter row. I think it was about Mum going to church, because it was the image of her, sitting on the edge of her bed pulling on her stockings getting ready for church, and crying, that has stuck in my mind. From then onwards, I understood that a deep gulf was fixed between my parents, and that they had to be regarded and treated in quite different ways.

Our nearest neighbours were both Italians. The Orlandis were about three hundred yards away, across Jefferson Road. This road, I hasten to explain, was named for a local timber-miller and brick-maker, not the former American President. The two Orlandi children were Louis and Frances, who were about Noel's age rather than mine, and Noel was three years older than I. They, especially Louis, were involved in some of our escapades later on. The Orlandis figured as items of my father's scorn, or at least Mr Orlandi did. He must have been on the dole, and my father would wax lyrical about the amount of money he received from the government, so much was it that he used to light his cigarettes with five-pound notes. I understand now that must have been said for dramatic effect, but for many years I regarded this accusation as being true, and would wonder how anyone could possibly do that. Images of smoke curling up from a burning five-pound note still come to me.

The Cafisos lived along Slaughterhouse Road a few hundred yards in the other direction. Mary Cafiso was my age, and I played with her a lot. The other three would be at school, and I would set off from home to walk to her place on my own, my mother waving from the front veranda. They don't let children roam about the countryside like that now. Mrs Cafiso had a beautiful and valuable collection of hand-worked linen she had brought out with her from Italy. There was a smell about the Cafiso household I can now identify as garlic, but then was a sign of difference that was important in my growing understanding of the world. I can remember that my understanding of the world was increased, also, by observing for the first time from Mary that girls were made differently from boys. The Cafisos' house was burnt down, and they went to live somewhere else, probably the Great Wen, Melbourne. The fire occurred on New Year's Day, and the whole town was at the sports at the football ground. I think it was a triangular contest between Garfield, Bunyip, and Nar Nar Goon. There came an announcement over the loudspeaker that there was a fire in that part of town, and all residents were advised to return home. We could see the ominous black cloud of smoke from the sports ground. When we got there, the house was utterly destroyed, and everything in it. Mrs Cafiso was missing, believed killed. A little later, Tessy, who was good at that sort of thing, found her sitting on the edge of the road, crying, a couple of hundred yards away. After that, the Cafisos vanished from our comprehension for ever.

We moved from there to the Lombardos'. More Italians. It's strange that we always refer to that house as Lombardo's, because they lived in it after we did, and not before. The house belonged to Mr Barker, and was on the main road between Garfield and the Princes Highway. It was actually set back from the road a hundred yards or so, and had a rough road – little more than a track - running beside it leading to another house behind ours, a quarter of a mile away. That road and that house became part of our lives a couple of years later, as I shall tell. The Lombardo's place had thirty acres, so Dad was able to get wood at the weekends, and there was grass for a cow, Darkie. After careful training from Noel ("Bend your knees as you land") I successfully jumped off the cowshed roof, a feat I then repeated for all visitors for the next year or so. The house was plain and simple. When you came in at the back, there was an enclosed dirt floor, which we took for granted, but which now seems extraordinary. No electricity or running water, of course.

Noel and I slept on the open front veranda, except that sometimes I slept in Dad's bed which was off the kitchen. The kitchen stove burnt morning, noon, and evening, summer and winter, and was the hub of our social activity. Each morning, Mum would scrape out the previous night's ashes and kindle the new fire. In the morning I would wake to the delicious smell of the fire's first smoke and the scraping and snapping of sticks, and the opening and closing of the fire-box as the flame was coaxed into life. In my half-conscious imaginings, this early morning ritual became a token of assurance for me in my dozy comfortableness, especially when the smell of toast and frying eggs reached me through the open door.

It was Noel's job to get the wood in each night, ready for the next morning, while I had to get the sticks. One night I forgot about the sticks. It must have been a weekend because Dad was home. He discovered my transgression after I had gone to bed, and I could hear him and Mum arguing about it. My mother's pleas on my behalf were of no avail, and I was ordered out of bed and to go and get the sticks in my pyjamas, barefoot on the wet ground, and in the dark. I groped around in the scrub for some sticks, reflecting bitterly on paternal cruelty and injustice.

When I was six and Noel nearly nine, Mum went to Melbourne for an operation, which meant she was away for six weeks. By then Dad had a job with the Forestry Commission and was away all week. So we four children had to be boarded out, and the house was shut up for the duration. Tessy, who was then thirteen, went to the Sturdys, Angela, aged twelve, to the Larsens out on the Swamp, while Noel and I stayed with the Misses McKay, two middle-aged spinsters who had the milk round in Garfield. Each morning they drove their horse and jinker round town filling up people's milk jugs left on the front veranda.

My young life was marked by a tendency to be led astray, chiefly by Noel. One day I joined an older and more criminal group of boys in breaking and entering Jack Manley's house on the Garfield Hill. Jack Manley was a funny old fellow who lived by himself. Perhaps we didn't break in; we just entered, when he was known to be absent. We rifled through his things. Well, the others did, while I watched. There was a pile of slips of paper, probably bank pay-in or withdrawal forms. We thought they were cheque forms. Just fill in the amount and get the money out at the bank. The others were whooping with joy. We would all be rich beyond our dreams. Just then, there was a footfall behind us. Jack was there. 'You boys just having a look around, are you?' he said, gently. I thought my life was over, but the others sweet-talked him, and we went off without further repercussions – except on my developing conscience!

A much larger episode of being led astray took place during the time of my mother's absence in hospital. The Misses McKay were busy at their work, and the head teacher at the school had other things to think about. So the fertile mind of my brother devised a splendid opportunity to dodge school. This we did for three consecutive weeks, which must surely be a record. We had no problem about going to school; the sheer challenge of beating the system was the attraction. Each day, we'd take our cut lunch, leave as if going to school, then head off to our various activities, like climbing Mount Cannibal, riding bikes out to the Main Drain, or raiding our own home to get potatoes to roast in a fire. We were Tom Sawyer and Huckleberry Finn all over again. The Orlandi children joined us some days. A lot of the time was spent in the pine plantation directly across the track from our house. It was the school plantation, by way of irony. Our adventure couldn't last. Someone in the line of authority twigged to it, and Noel, unfortunately for him, took the rap.

Our neighbours were a little closer than at Webb's. The Blackwells, about two hundred yards away, we knew best. Mr Blackwell was killed in an accident in Northern Australia, working with heavy machinery, during the war. Mrs Blackwell married again and became Mrs Fenn, but Mr Fenn disappeared very soon afterwards, so that left Mrs Blackwell, now Mrs Fenn, with the seven children. They ranged from Tessy's age to down below me. Pax and Pearl were friends of Tessy and Angela. Angela could call out to them from our place and they would call back. Noel rather missed out on having a companion Blackwell, but Geoff, the next, was my age, and he and his brothers, Alan and Cliff, were good friends. For the record, Beryl and Evelilith filled out the Blackwell stable. There were good times at the Blackwells' place. Some of their friends would come as well. One day, there was a heap of Blackwells and Connellys and others playing in their front yard, when a car passed slowly along the road, the passengers looking out at us all in wonderment. Someone yelled out to them, 'Not all the same family, mate'. It broke us all up.

I started school at four and a half, in 1938. The first day, I went home at lunch-time, thinking school was over for the day, which was a sign I shouldn't perhaps have been there in the first place. I came to regret that I was so young as against virtually all of my classmates throughout my twelve years of schooling. The teacher when I began was Miss Maynard, who was the first woman I'd noticed to have bulges in the upper front part of her body. What with Mary Cafiso and Miss Maynard, I was learning about life. For my fifth birthday, my mother gave me a pants suit. It had four button-up pockets, two in the shirt part and two in the pants part. Mum had Mrs Mason make it up. Mrs Mason was the housekeeper for Mr Robinson up on the highway – the same Mr Robinson as gave us the cricket bat. We used it for years, even when it was split and splintered. In fact, I think it's still around somewhere. A number of men had housekeepers in those days, but my learning of life did not allow me to draw the conclusions then that I would draw nowadays. The great pleasure of this birthday gift, the pants suit, was that there was a penny in each pocket. My own money!

There were many embarrassments to be endured. Mum once got me to recite a poem for Mr Simcocks in his shop, and I was given a double-headed ice-cream as a reward. I hated doing it, but I knew Mum wanted me to. Our class put on a play for the end of term and the mothers came to watch us. The play was 'Snow White and the Seven Dwarfs'. I was one of the dwarfs. Just as the play started my mask slipped over my face, and I went through the whole performance as though blindfolded. Perhaps the parents were amused, but I was marked for ever! My life was governed by what others thought of me or what they might think of me. Where were the school psychologists when I needed them? One day, in Dandenong with Mum, she wanted to buy me a new pencil sharpener. There were dozens of them out on display, of every fancy shape and colour, Mum urging me to choose one of the fancy ones. I chose the plainest, greyest one there, to my mother's clear disappointment, but I couldn't tell her that the other kids might have laughed at me if I had chosen a bright and 'childish' one.

Some people, great men and women in particular, in their early years, show indications of their later life work in the idle passions they develop. That hasn't worked for me. The only great passion I had was for racehorses. I suppose it came from Dad, who followed the horses and the boxing and wrestling, all on radio. Can you imagine listening to wrestling on the wireless? That was a regular part of our Friday and Saturday nights entertainment. But it was the horses that got into me. I studied the form guide in the Sun. I knew all the jockeys' names. Barrier positions and weights were my meat and drink, though handicapping I never quite mastered. When a race was on, I'd sit astride the arm of the sofa and whip my chosen horse home just as vigorously as its jockey was doing at the same moment. At one of the concerts in the Hall, I once – perhaps twice- did a phantom call of the Melbourne Cup before it was actually run, without notes, relying entirely on memory for the horses' and jockeys' names. As for picking winners, I did that all the time. Once my mother, impressed by my skill, asked which horse was most likely to win on that Saturday. I replied, immediately, 'Dornford, in the last race.' Without telling me, she asked Mr Conlin, on his way to the pub, to put two shillings on it. This, I might say, was the one and only wager ever to be conducted in the Connelly household. Late that night, Mr Conlin returned with seven and six for Mum. Dornford had won at five to two. The money went into housekeeping! [P.S Dr Google has since told me that Dornford, a gelding, was sired by the champion, Windbag, who won the Melbourne Cup in 1926. Dornford later switched to hurdles with great success]

Dad was very anxious about fires. He insisted on the fire in the open fireplace in the main room being put out each night, to be re-lit the next day. Fires were more common then. Houses were mostly built of timber, and everyone had wood fires in their house. Three shops in the main street were burnt down before we came to Garfield, and later the hotel and the Hall, as well, separately. And the Cafisos'. While we were at Lombardos', the terrible fires of Black Friday, 1939, occurred. They came close to us. Cinders were landing around our house and we had fun stamping on them and putting them out. Another year, there was a bad fire in the forest north of Garfield. Cliff Pringle, the policeman, who later was our football coach, went down to the hotel and ordered all the drinkers out and told them to go and fight the fire.

There were tragedies in the town, which engendered a vague feeling of the fragility of life in me and perhaps in others. Mrs Perkins from Garfield North, whose daughter came to school with us, was killed when the jinker she was driving down the Garfield Hill crashed at the bottom of the hill, where the road curves sharply to the left. The horse had bolted when a boy innocently cracked a stock whip behind one of the houses. Mr Callinan, who ran a saw mill half way up the hill, was killed when a chip struck him in the neck. A boy we went to school with was drowned in a well a few years later, and there were dark mutterings about the cause of it. Charlie Grey's daughter caught some rare and lingering disease that the doctors were unable to identify, let alone cure. The little boy from one of the grocer's shops was killed on the railway line when he wandered away. What hit us hardest, however, was a terrible event up near the highway, when some of the young men were drinking and fooling around. One of them was shot dead. Afterwards, the fellow who did it was out on bail and drowned himself.

All these people were well known to us. In Garfield at that time, everyone knew everyone else, either directly or through town gossip. Awful events like these added to the element of bare coarseness that seems, to me at least, to have hung over the town. The talk amongst the bigger boys at school, for instance, was often very rough. Once, I remember, when one of these bigger kids had made some crude sexual remark, Mr Chappell, the teacher, who came up behind him at that instant, gave him a slap on the head and said, 'I'll have none of that sort of talk here.' I was a silent observer of this scene and it made a deep mark on me.

Later on, I remember a group of us scouts riding in the back of the scoutmaster, Bill Parish's, utility, all, except me, singing crude songs at the top of their voices. This coarseness was something I couldn't identify when I was young, and I might be wrong about it, but, I believe that, nevertheless, the distaste for it got into my bones to some extent. Our family was not like that! I grew up with a sense of being different from the general run of the people and families around me. Garfield belonged to me, but did I belong to Garfield? I've recently come across a piece by an English writer describing his boyhood where he expresses much that was also in my forming mind. His mother forbade him to go and play with "the village children". He writes, "In no uncertain terms it announced that my lot would be to stand behind a wall of separating glass, on the outside, looking in; a spectator, not an actor, excluded from the enviable society on the street." In my case, so much as I felt a wall of glass between me and my peers, it was a wall of my own making. Even living a distance from the street, up above the township, became a symbol of this difference.

But cheerfulness always wins out in the end! Our time at Lombardos' was rounded off with a happy event – my seventh birthday. Five or six other children came, though I can remember only two of them, and that's because I still have the book they gave me, The Heroes by Charles Kingsley, about the Greek myths. I've written in the front, 'For my seventh birthday, from Ian and Peter Paterson'. Dr Paterson was the doctor in Garfield. The party was a Cowboys and Indians party. We all dressed up in moleskins, or the best approach to moleskins that our mothers could rustle up, and fired toy pistols at one another.

Chapter 2

Sometime in the latter part of 1940, we left Lombardos'. It happened in this way. We knew the Pratt family well, from church – Mr and Mrs Pratt, Jim, Nancy, and Tom. Mum and Mrs Pratt were particularly good friends. The Pratts, I realise now, were comfortably off. They had a good farm out on the Swamp on a rare piece of rising ground known as Governor's Hill because the Governor of Victoria, Sir Henry Loch, used to come there in the 1880s to shoot ducks. The Pratts had a nice car, a Chevrolet, number plate 66 461. (I've always had a head for figures). The 30-acre block immediately behind our place at Lombardos', with a large house, better than most houses round about, came up for sale, and the Pratts bought it. I think the price was £750. They did this solely for us. We moved straight in and paid it off at five pounds a month, without interest.

We called the place, 'Winston', unsurprisingly for 1940. The Battle for Britain was raging about the same time we moved in. We were now a little further from the street – about a twenty-minute walk. This was the family home for the next seventeen years, even long after the four children had individually left it. Indeed, if I had now to name a place that was my spiritual home, this would be it. I can walk over every inch of house and land in my mind's eye, with perfect remembering. Although it was a large house, there weren't many bedrooms. Tessy and Angela slept in Mum's room, while Noel and I had a sleep-out beside the house, where we shared a double bed. Dad's room was off the kitchen-dining room. The bathroom was at the end of the front veranda. For our baths, we would heat water in kerosene tins on the stove and carry them to the bath. There was an attic, but there was no way to get to it without scaling the side of the chimney, getting on the roof of the kitchen, and climbing though a small window up above. Still, it was a delightful retreat, safe from parents, and even siblings couldn't approach without being heard far off.

Still no mains water, nor electricity. We lit the house and did our homework by the light of an Aladdin pressure lantern, or, when that failed, kerosene lamps or candles. Replacing mantles and trimming wicks were part of our set of life skills. We had a cool cupboard in the middle of the house, that is, a square space running from the earthen area under the floorboards up to the attic, so there was a cool upward draft all the time. With that and a Koolgardie safe on the veranda, we kept the meat and the milk and the butter and the jellies cool and firm, to a degree. After some years, we bought a kerosene refrigerator, which was placed in the large sitting room as there was no other place it could go. Mum had a table cut in half for a kitchen work bench, and, for water, there was a single cold tap over the sink. In dry seasons, the thousand-gallon tank outside would run low and we would anxiously tap it each day to discover the water level. If it did run dry, there was a well alongside, with an ancient hand-pump and a pipe going down to the murky and fearsome depths below.

Dad had been on sustenance in the late 'thirties, digging out drains around the town, for one thing. Sometimes I would go down after school to join him. Once, near the football ground, he disturbed a snake in the gutter and finished him off with his shovel. Afterwards we walked home together, Dad wheeling his bike up the hill. By now, however, Dad had a permanent job with the Forestry Commission. The start of the War meant that men could gain employment more easily. He spent the week, from dark on Monday morning to dark on Friday night, away at his camp at Gentle Annie, a mountain in the Black Snake Ranges, north of Labertouche, some thirty-five kilometres away. He'd pack his sugar-bag with his provisions – corned beef, bread, butter, potatoes, sugar, tea – tie it up by looping the rope from one of the bottom corners round the top of the bag, and have enough slack to sling the bag over his shoulder, and set off, walking down to the end of the road or else to the street in Garfield to be picked up by his boss. He lived an utterly lonely life at Gentle Annie, keeping the road and the telephone line clear, checking the logs being taken out by truck, and spotting fires in summer. The three men each had their own little hut, furnished with bush timber. I went to stay with him for the week several times in the school holidays. Once, on a high fire danger day, I had to walk two miles down the road to call a work gang back to the depot. It was hot! They misunderstood the message, and I returned without them. So I had to go again … and back! I remember the dank earthy smell of the bush as I walked.

At the camp-site the men had a deep underground dug-out they could get into in case of bushfire. Dad gave me a treat by making a jelly and putting it in the cool bunker to set. When I came to get it, there was a huge snake on the bottom step of the entrance, which promptly disappeared into the blackness of the dug-out's interior. One of the men came with a flame-thrower which lit up the interior of the bunker. He located the snake and torched it to death as I watched in horror.

At home, the economic plan was that Dad would bring home his pay from the Forestry, while Mum would make money from the chooks we kept. There were vegetables from the garden at times, and plenty of apples from nearby orchards in season. One year, Mum planted out a huge bed of strawberries in the hope of making money, but that came to nothing in the end. The chooks played a big part in our lives. There were three hundred of them, white leghorns, which everybody kept in those days. No exotic breeds then, nor heavy-laying breeds like Isa Browns. The eggs were packed into large wooden boxes which were picked up each Tuesday morning by a truck from the Egg Board. Some were destined for export to Britain, and we would sit up at night smearing them with Kepeg so they would last the journey. The chooks were let out each morning, and some were occasionally taken by foxes, while a ferret got into one of the sheds one night and killed a dozen or more. Once our two dogs went mad and killed a whole lot, so, "once a killer, always a killer", they had to be put down, and after the manner of things in those days, that meant Bill Parish came one Saturday morning with his shot gun, took the dogs up into the bush, and shot them. I heard the shots as I lay cringing in bed. It was a raw upbringing for children in those days! The chooks came as day-old sexed chicks, 100 at a time, in a large, flat cardboard box, to the railway station, where we'd pick them up and carry them home. They'd be put in a brooder in one of the chook sheds, kept warm by means of a kerosene burner in the centre of their little lodging house until they could get about a bit. Their first feed – and this was Dad's special knowledge – was charcoal, to clear their gut out. For the first few weeks they had a special pelletised grain called chickfeed. Quite a few died, and some turned out to be roosters. The birds began to lay after about twenty weeks. It was Mum who had the job of caring for them, with the help of us kids. They were fed wheat and mash – pollard and bran mixed by hand – with a dash of shell grit added, especially when some soft-shelled eggs would appear.

The feed came from Bunyip. On a Saturday morning, Dad would harness the horse up to the old cart, which looked very much as though it might fall apart at any moment, and go off, usually with Noel and me aboard, to Permewan Wright's, taking the old road north of the railway line rather than the busier road on the other side of the line. We'd always look out for a crumbling old place beside the road about half-way between Garfield and Bunyip. It was collapsing into the ground, and had a faded sign in front – 'Home Sweet Home'. There was something of infinite sadness about it, and it's always been for me a symbol of "change and decay in all around I see".

They lived, these leghorns, in six sheds, fifty to each shed, arranged around the two sides of an open space fifty yards across. The chook sheds were numbered 1 to 6, and there was a seventh shed, 'Number 7', a double-storied bush-built barn used as a storage and hay shed. The dray was kept there, and a jinker, though the jinker was never used, probably because we didn't have a suitable horse to go with it. We had a separate feed shed as well, where the cow and chook feed was kept, together with tools. The chook sheds were made of bush timber and corrugated iron, wire netting on the front, with earthen floors covered by chook litter. The roosts were sawn timber boards hung from the ceiling by fencing wire. The nest boxes were in a series of six boxes, cut from kerosene tins, nailed together on timber boards, and laid on the ground. They were infested by rats, so every now and then we would have a rat hunt. These were very important in building family togetherness. On a Saturday morning, we all, except for Mum, armed ourselves with killing sticks, and surrounded the row of nest boxes. After a dramatic countdown, Dad would lift up the nests, exposing the rats, which we flailed to death. That done, we moved on to the next shed. It was on one of these occasions I made my first joke. We were waiting for the slaughter to begin, when I said to the others, 'I'm thirsty', then, in a moment of inspiration, I added, 'bloodthirsty'. Everyone laughed. A big boost for a small boy!

Despite all these goings on at home, we were people of the town as well. Later, when I was at university and read Browning's poem, 'Up at a Villa, down in the City', it reverberated with me, because that's just how it was in my mind back in those early Garfield days. We'd leave our stronghold, high over the town above the steep Garfield Hill, and descend to the metropolis, where a different kind of life was celebrated. There was the town and there was us. I was very conscious of the distinction. We'd leave our place to go to the pictures or the doctor's or to get a haircut or to get the wet battery charged for the wireless, or to post a letter or to catch the train. Then we'd return to our stronghold. Always walking of course, and carrying things home with us (though there was a weekly delivery of the major shopping items.)

Sometimes now, at night, I'm there again in memory, walking down into Garfield. I have total recall of it. We walk along the front paddock, past the two telephone poles, through the gate, turn right up that steepish embankment into the bush (whose bush?; we never knew nor asked!), striking up the gentle slope of the hill. There's a left turn, then a right, where the scrub opens out and there are patches of fog grass. Here the track splits in two for fifty or sixty yards before emerging into clearer country. It's a single track and we walk in Indian file. Now we join a wider path coming down from Phillips's fence. If we turned right here, we could climb over the stile and visit Jack and Jean Phillips and their son, John, but we swing left and downhill instead, curving right through taller timber until we come to the Big Tree. We might hide something here, in the hollow at the back, for someone else in the family to collect, or if it was heavy, for them to carry the rest of the way. We come to the narrow path running alongside Barker's Road, and then across it, cutting off the corner, past that soggy part where a spring leaks from the ground and those greenhood orchids grow in their masses. (This is where I once hid in the scrub while Angela and Noel walked past on their way home from High School, and came out, by pre-arrangement, to join Tessy who had loitered behind, the two of us walking home in blissful companionship). Now we're on the main gravel road, and it's straight downhill, across the railway line, and into town. There are only two people in the world, now, who have all this in their mind. Soon there will be one, and then none. All knowledge of these memories will be lost to the world. Not an easy thought to bear, but it's the way of all things, I suppose.

Chapter 3

The main street of Garfield is exactly the same now as it was seventy years ago. There should be a heritage order placed on it as a living souvenir of past times. The doctor's house was a little apart from the shops, a double-story building, as seemed appropriate. It was just opposite where the new bridge over the railway line has been built. The Post Office was the first of the shops, at the Bunyip end of town. In my early days, it was kept by the fearsome Mrs Drayson. Mail was kept in little pigeon-holes, A to Z, and we'd ask for it at the counter. Sometimes, if there were adults who came in after me, Mrs Drayson would serve them first, but I accepted this with equanimity as just the way of the world for small children. Every Thursday there was a tiny package of yeast from Melbourne for Mum to bake bread with. Stamps were twopence each. On the back wall was a poster about putting the correct stamp on letters. *"Oh dear, fourpence tax. How annoying!"* a woman was saying, who'd forgotten to put a stamp on her letter. Behind the partition we could hear the girl on the switchboard putting callers through on the manual exchange. She had a funny way of saying, 'Hello'. It sounded like 'Hollyhock'. Or perhaps 'Hollyhock' was the Garfield Exchange call sign. I could never work it out. Next door was the police station, transferred from alongside the school on the other side of the line. There was a large garden in front of the policeman's home. Our schoolyard gossip was that policemen were required to do hard manual work to keep them fit. I wonder how many of these half-formed imaginings of ours were true. Next came Jimmy Dean's garage, then Wall's baker's shop - white bread always, smelling delicious, and wrapped in tissue paper, and sold in two sizes - half a loaf or a large loaf. Mostly, Mum baked our own, of course. Next, across the side-road, was Eric Edis's blacksmith shop. After school we'd gather at the entrance to watch him shoeing mighty, stamping horses, swearing savagely at them all the while. He'd pump the bellows and the coals would glow. He'd take a horseshoe out of the coals and bash it into shape with his hammer, the sparks flying. He'd plunge it into the cold water with a great fizz of steam.

The picture theatre was alongside. There were films every Saturday night, and everybody seemed to go. Sometimes Noel and I went without any money. Noel was adept at attaching himself to a large family party and walking in undetected. Jimmy Fawkner, our football captain, had a butcher's shop next door to the theatre, then came Jack and Jean Phillips' soft goods shop, where I worked when I was old enough on Christmas Eve, to help with the rush. The Phillips were friends of ours. They lived next to us, only a few hundred yards away. Alongside the Phillips' shop was a private house where the Jonases lived. Next was Barneses' sweet shop (how could they make a living in that tiny place?), and then came our neighbour, Mr Lombardo's, barber's shop. To cut my hair, he'd put a square box on his chair so that I was high enough. If you walked through a passage-way you came to the billiard saloon, attached to the barber's shop. I could hear the click of the balls as I sat in the chair, but never ventured into the room itself, which seemed slightly exotic and dangerous.

Mr Lombardo met with a near-disaster about this time. The family went to visit the Buchan Caves further up in Gippsland. After the gates were locked for the night, Mr Lombardo was found to be missing. He'd been locked inside, but was soon rescued and saved from a cold and lonely night. Mr Simcocks' shop was next in line, the hub of the town. He sold newspapers, ice cream, and tobacco amongst other things. Sometimes I would buy Dad's tobacco for him. Mr Simmy, as he was known, would pull it out, surreptitiously, from under the counter, because it was in short supply during the war. If there was someone he wasn't sure about in the shop at the time, he'd wait till they'd gone before he served me. Two ounces of Havelock ready-rubbed and a packet of Tally-ho cigarette papers was the usual order.

There were two grocer's shops – Nutting's, then Edney's a little further along. There didn't seem much difference, except that Nutting's sold Bushells tea and Edney's sold Robur. Nevertheless, the town was divided in its support for either place. Johnny Edney was in my grade at school. He had a little black mark beneath his left eye that looked for all the world like the point of a back-lead pencil that had somehow become lodged under the skin. We'd speculate for hours about this phenomenon, but no one felt able to ask him about it. We dealt with Nutting's, because we knew them well. Beth Nutting was a friend of Tessy's and Robert Nutting later came to live with us for six months as a war evacuee from Melbourne after the Nuttings moved away. They bought a historic home in Black Rock – Black Rock House – and we children stayed there sometimes. When

Noel and I went, Mr Nutting would have jobs ready for us, like hacking though the base of a huge Moreton Bay fig so he could gain a back access to his garage. He was a hard man.

Between the grocers' shops was the Bank – the English, Scottish and Australian, ESA. Here I opened my first bank account. We would talk about how the manager slept with a loaded revolver under his pillow. Maybe it was true. There was a vacant block, then came Keith Sarah, the chemist, then another sweet shop run by Mr and Mrs Whelan, and a second butcher's shop, Con Breman's, who played cricket with us. The Iona Hotel, down at the lower end of the street, was to me a place of mystery and danger. Strange things were said to occur there, and there was the sour smell of beer as we walked past. None of us ever went into the pub, except Noel, after he started to play football. There was no alcohol at home. Almost at the end of the street was Mr Interlighi, who was the boot-maker. He was regarded with some suspicion during the war years. The Italian prisoners-of-war who worked on the asparagus farm on the Swamp used to congregate at his shop at the weekends. Last of all, near the corner with the Thirteen-

Mile Road, was Hams' garage, which was taken over by Jack Brenchley about the time the war ended.

Across the road from the street was the railway station. In wartime, it was browned-out like all the houses, and there were posters warning against careless talk. *'The Walls have Ears,'* one proclaimed. If we were going to Melbourne to see Aunty Vivien in Caulfield or Aunty Janet in St Albans or to go to the football, say, we'd catch the ten-to-seven train. In winter, it would still be dark, and the lights of the approaching train and the sparks flying and the deep growl of the engine would excite my imagination beyond words.

Across the railway line was Parish's packing shed. After school, a lot of us would hang round the large open side of the shed as the packers filled the boxes with amazing dexterity. The apples ran along a roller and fell into one of several bins according to how large they were and the gap allowed for them to fall through. A row of packers stood, one at each bin. They'd grasp each apple, wrap it in tissue with a flick of the wrist and set it in its patterned place in the wooden case. I was fascinated by the packers and by the equipment. I suppose it was the first piece of machinery I'd ever seen, at least at close quarters. After half an hour or so, Mr Parish would come and toss us some apples and we'd go away. On one side of the packing shed, jammed into the corner of the main road, was the Baby Health Centre, and on the other side was the Hall. Every now and then, dances were held on Friday nights, sometimes big occasions with a band, and sometimes a smaller occasion to encourage the teenagers, with just Mrs Bassed on the piano. Before the dance began, sawdust was sprinkled over the floor, then swept off, to make a fast surface. A church group of mysterious origin met at the Hall on Sundays. How could you have church in a hall, I wondered? During the week, their sign propped in a front window read, '*The Gospel will be preached here, if the Lord wills, on Sunday next at 2.00 p.m.*' This greatly puzzled me. I was not familiar with the theology implied there. Further on from the Hall, in a line above the railway line, was first the school, and then, after a couple of houses, the church. St Mary's Church of England. Our church. After that the road to Tynong began.

Chapter 4

More than half of our land was cleared, so we could have two cows and a draught horse as well. When one of the cows went dry, Andy Duncan would come and take it to the bull at his place out on the Thirteen-Mile Road on the Swamp, and bring it back a week or so later. Ten shillings was the fee. Andy was one of the town's characters. He was a cattle dealer, given to much bad language, and rode his horse everywhere, in all weathers, in his great rainproof coat. Once we sold a cow at the Dandenong market. One of the cattle trucks, Calvert's, probably, picked it up, and took it down to Dandenong. I rode down in the cab and represented the cow in the saleyard. When it came into the ring, I was alongside the auctioneer, muttering in his ear things like, "Very quiet." "Fed on grass." "Hand-reared," and he was passing all this on to the excited bidders. I think we got a fair price, in the end. It was a good growing-up experience for me.

Dad, with Noel's help, planted a crop of potatoes once or twice, and maize another year. I was too small to do anything except occasionally drive the horse while Dad or

Noel managed the single-furrow plough, but Noel was quite magnificent. With Dad away at work, he single-handedly ploughed the whole of the middle paddock, two or three acres in area. He was probably eleven or twelve at the time. One of my keenest memories is of Dad sowing millet by hand in the paddock just below the house, Biblical fashion, casting the seed right-hand then left-hand from the cutaway wheat bag slung across his stomach and fixed by being tied behind his shoulders.

We had another horse at times, one for us to ride. One of these ponies was called Buttons, a wretch of a thing which might be cajoled and kicked to take us down to the far end of the front paddock, then would canter back to home, the pleasure of that hardly worth the effort of the first half of the journey. One day, George Edwards, who was the minister at the church at that time, came to visit us. It must have been in the holidays, because I was home. In my endeavour to show off to our esteemed visitor - I was born under the sign of Leo, and thus have ever sought the limelight! – I mounted this steed and forced him to the end of the paddock, then, with Mum and Mr Edwards watching this superb feat of horsemanship, I turned the horse's head and set sail at a glorious gallop towards home. Right in front of them, the wretched beast stopped dead and put his head down, sending me flying off, mortified, their laughter echoing in my ears. Another, bigger, horse we bought from Clive Smith, up on the highway. I was deputed to fetch him, which meant walking the two miles to the Smith's, then riding him home along the highway, a venture unimaginable these days. Once or twice I rode him down the street to do the shopping, dismounting and tying him up to the veranda posts just like in the westerns. I felt like John Wayne.

A lot of time I spent simply wandering over our new place. There were kangaroos, snakes, echidnas, kookaburras, magpies, blue wrens, heath, wattle, and orchids. Dorothea McKellar could have written 'My Country' at our place. In January, the blackberry season would start. Mum's apple pies became apple and blackberry pies. The mushrooms appeared when the first good rains came after the summer dry spell. We'd go far and wide after them. I'm a hunter-and-gatherer by nature! In spare moments, I might head off down through the side bush which Dad once burnt as a bush fire precaution, as it was on the north-western side of the house. Then through an open gateway into the side paddock, where we often saw the kangaroos, sometimes two of them standing up and boxing each other, and where we often set the rabbit traps. This gave way to the bottom paddock which was my favourite part. The western end was covered by scattered ti-tree regrowth about eight feet high, but the grass beneath had retained its soft springiness. I could hide here and nobody would know where I was. It was here that Mum came after a bitter scene at home, and she fled, sobbing, she knew not where. But I knew, or I sensed, where she would go, and some little time later, I went after her, found her there amongst the ti-tree, and brought her home.

Further along, the bottom paddock was low-lying and swampy. Dad had ideas about draining it, but they never came to anything. It was near here that I had two snake experiences. One was the killing of my first snake. Poor thing; it was curled up asleep and had no chance. I had time to go all the way home to get the shovel; it was still sleeping there when I got back. Another time I saw an albino snake nearby. There was an old car tyre lying in the scrub. I poked at it with a stick and a pure white snake came slithering out of it and away. I thought at first it was a giant earthworm – there are such creatures in Gippsland – but it travelled so fast it must have been a snake, I concluded.

The bush on the eastern side of the farm was more open and scrubby. The big timber had been cleared long since. We could make out the line where the tramline had been laid years before to cart the wagons of timber, horse-drawn, from North Garfield down to the old Cannibal Creek siding on the railway line. There was a very small and shallow dam here amongst the stunted trees. One day there was a tremendous rain and hail storm. It broke windows all over the town and was written up in the 'Sun'. I was walking home from school when it happened and I ran on to Edis's front veranda to escape death by stoning. When it stopped and I got home, I found that the flooding rain had carried light objects to all points of the place, and this small dam was completely filled with hailstones that had washed into it. I could walk across the dam on the hailstones. It was just up from here, years later, when I was fifteen and sixteen, I spent aching weeks and months pulling stumps out of the ground with a trewhella jack. I had visions of turning this barren land into smiling pasture, but like so many of my projects it came to nothing.

Dad, with Noel's help, would fell a couple of trees for firewood and cart it up to the woodshed on a sledge he had made, drawn by the horse. Later I learnt that these sledges were common in Ireland in the nineteenth century, and I feel sure that Dad's sledge was a direct carry-over from his Irish background. All the bush work was done with an axe. I can't work out why we never used a saw. We needed a lot of wood. As well as the kitchen stove, there were the two open fires, in the small sitting room and the large sitting room. The getting of sufficient wood was a major element in our annual work schedule, and this is where Dad came into his own. He knew about trees and axes and how to fell trees and how to stack wood. He taught Noel and me about getting wood as other fathers teach their sons how to fish.

The cowshed was built of round bush timber covered in sheets of bark. Dad was very good at barking timber, and we boys also became expert. The cow would lazily chew away at its bran, leg-roped, head locked into the bail, while one of us – this was a task shared around the family, though it was always Mum on school days – would milk it into a bucket, head comfortably nestled against the warm flank of the cow. A good place to dream! Mum would scald the excess milk in a basin on top of the stove; the cream would rise to the top, and be scooped off to make butter. The butter-making was at first done by hand, relentless beating eventually persuading the cream to 'turn', always just when one's wrists were at breaking point. Later we had a separator to separate the cream from the milk, and also a wooden churn to do the actual butter-making. The cowshed was built alongside a row of very large pine trees. Noel and I were as agile and fearless as monkeys as we swung ourselves around in the topmost branches.

There was thick bush behind our land, as well, and we had uninhibited access to that. There were wide tracks running through it, and we could walk through this bush to the Parish's place or the Sturdys', or else to play on the huge, moss-covered granite rock faces that covered large areas of ground. We went barefoot most of the time. All my life I've advocated going barefoot when young as the recipe for a long and healthy life. There's an acute contra-indication here, actually, as I was terrified of snakes. Not now, but then. Sometimes, if on a path surrounded by long grass, I would stand petrified for five or ten minutes when I heard a sound in the grass ahead, waiting and hoping for the snake to go away. Then I'd run at top speed through the danger area, my heart in my mouth. My scheming brother always made me walk in front of him in the bush. One day I said to him, 'I know why you do this. It's so I'll be bitten by the snake and not you.' 'Not so,' he replied. 'I'm doing it for your protection. You'll wake the snake up, and it will be just ready to bite when I reach it.' I was too young to see through this sophistry. Despite such fears and experiences, I'm sure my life-long need to own a block of land stems partly from this early experience of living close to the bush – as well as from my Irish ancestry.

On Sunday afternoons, we went to church. Well, Mum and we kids did. That meant walking down our track, up and then down-hill through Phillips' place, along Barker's Road for a bit, then plunging down steeply through the bush behind the church. We might have a ride home, however, to the end of our lane in Mr Bassed's huge old canvas-covered tourer, with its two internal dickie-seats, facing backwards. The church was quite new, built in 1935. When it was pulled down and the land sold half a century later, I grieved deeply, especially when I went there and found cigarette butts and empty beer cans scattered around the house that was built in its place.

The Sunday service was always at half past two, so it was nearly always Evening Prayer, not Holy Communion. Mr and Mrs Bassed sat near the back, not far from Mr and Mrs Laity, who lived near them in Garfield North. Mr and Mrs Moore and their daughter, Phyllis, were also at the back.

Mrs Parish played the organ, Mr Parish and Bill alongside her, and Mr Parish's brother, 'Unk' sitting next. The five Pratts sat on the other side from us – Jim, Nancy, and Tom, bookended by Mrs Pratt against the wall and Mr Pratt on the aisle. Mr Pratt took up the collection during the final hymn. He waited until the last verse had begun, when he nonchalantly folded up his glasses, picked up the collection plate and slowly moved through the church with studied ease, while I was in an agony of anxiety whether he would finish before the hymn ended. His timing was always perfect. We sat in the first pew inside the door with Mrs Sippo. In summer, the door would be open, and there came the pleasant sound of the outside world, birds and distant cars, and –is this my imagination? – of murmuring bees. Church was a comfortable place. The liturgy was the same each week; the people were the same; they were all people I was pleased to be with; the ministers said comfortable things. When I didn't understand something, I didn't fret. All would make sense when I came to greater maturity. Are children these days so ready to wait for things, to accept their childish level of understanding?

One summer holidays, I went to a church camp for boys on Raymond Island in East Gippsland. The only thing I remember is that I was at the height of my cricket passion, and I became the demon bowler who took all the wickets in our cricket matches. Life at St Mary's was wonderfully predictable ... or usually so. One day the minister was in the middle of his sermon. He was speaking about how earthly things fade away; only things of the Spirit last for ever. "Why," he said, "the great Roman Empire crumbled away; the Greeks before that; even our great British Empire will one day fade away to nothing." At that there was a noisy intervention from the side of the church. Mrs Parish, at the organ, English-born and a fervent imperialist, drew herself up to her full height and declared, "Never! Never! Never!" and sat down again. For me, it was as though the earth had stopped spinning. I was aghast. Somehow the minister stumbled on to an early conclusion to his sermon.

When I was fourteen, I was confirmed by the Bishop, Donald Burns Blackwood, a very austere figure, he seemed to me. It was in our own church, though I think some young people from Bunyip were in the group as well, and perhaps Nar Nar Goon, as that was also in our Parish. After the service, we were gathered in the vestry where the Bishop gave us a talk on the evils of alcohol, and, exploiting the raised good intentions of the day, persuaded us all to sign the pledge, which he passed around from one to another. We all duly signed ... except for one strong and determined figure, my brother, Noel, who refused. I was amazed and deeply impressed. We all sensed the manipulation that was going on, but only Noel acted upon it. Nevertheless, I do remember walking home afterwards, by myself, the long way round, in something of a cloud of spiritual uplift.

Chapter 5

The Sippos lived a mile or so out of Garfield on the Swamp, next to Andy Duncan, the cattle dealer, and the new slaughter-house. Later the Garfield golf course was built on this land. Mrs Sippo was as thin as a telephone pole, rather like Mum, and walked everywhere. She and Mum were thrown together quite a lot because of their church connection. Mrs Pratt was the third member of a close triumvirate. I seemed to be at the Sippos' place quite often, one way or another. Mrs Sippo had the distinction of being the only person we knew who drank coffee rather than tea as a matter of custom. She made her coffee by putting a teaspoonful of a horrible oily brown substance called coffee chicory in the bottom of a cup and filling it with hot water. She gave me some once. Never again! There were two Sippo children, Bill and Olive. Bill was in Tessy's year at High School and went on to be a Patrol Officer in New Guinea. Olive later worked as the telephone operator at the Post Office. Mr Sippo, Les, who was of Scandinavian background, worked with his brother, Dook, who lived with them, in building and repairing bridges all over the district, just as their father had done before them. They had an old tourer car to take them to work. Miss Redmond was a cousin who also came to live in what must have been a crowded house. Against Mrs Sippo's beanpole structure, Miss Redmond was a beer barrel. In school one day, Mr Chappell was teaching us about the rivers of North America, and he referred, with a knowing and guilty look on his face, to the 'Mississippo and Miss Sour-eye'. We all knew who he was talking about.

We sometimes went to the pictures on Saturday nights. The first film I ever saw, or the first I remember seeing, was 'The Wizard of Oz.' I was terrified as Dorothy and another person made their way along a tree-lined road, as one after the other, the evil trees crashed to the road attempting to smash them to pieces, the two of them barely escaping each time. We'd get home from the pictures late and have a cup of cocoa with Mum, prepared on a little methylated spirits stove, the fire having gone out long before. I suppose I got my craze for guns (not real ones) from the westerns at the theatre. These guns always brought me grief, however. I had a wonderful wooden rifle – a piece of cast-off building plank, actually – but it had a sharp point like a bayonet and a square cut out in the right place for the trigger, and even a nail for a trigger. I played with it for what seems like years. I loved it more than life itself. Then one day it was missing. Dad had chopped it up for the fire. Mum remonstrated with him, and he said, 'It was only a piece of wood.' Later, I was given the most beautiful revolver with a pearl handle. One day I hid it in the bush for some reason I can't remember, and when I went back for it the next day it was gone. Did other children have such griefs to bear?

I'd be highly excited when we played games at night or on rainy weekends. There were card games like fish when we were young, and pelmanism (they call it 'Memory' now), but we soon graduated to euchre and five hundred, and also to crib. When I was probably thirteen I went to one of the regular euchre evenings in the supper room of the Hall, and played a bad lead. My partner – a middle-aged matron of the town - was furious, and I never went back again! But the games I most enjoyed – and still look back on as a symbol of the lost innocence of childhood – were the ones that involved acting. The best of these was charades (pronounced *charardes*, please!), where one team, say Tessy and Noel and I, would think of a three-syllable word, each syllable itself being a word or sounding like one (e.g. air-oh-plain = aeroplane). Then we'd act out three scenes, where one of us would use one of these short words, before a final act where we had to use the whole word, using all the long words we could possibly think of in order to confuse the other team. Then, the others, in this case, Mum and Angela, after trying to guess our word, would have their turn.

Dumb Crambo was another favourite. It was rather like charades, except that in this case one team would act out in dumb show a word, where they had previously given a rhyming word to the opposition as a clue. Then there was Up Jenkins, which no googling will ever discover for you. With Up Jenkins, there are two teams, one on either side of the table. The first side would take a threepenny bit and wedge it cunningly behind one of their thumbs so that it couldn't be seen from across the table. When ready, on the command, 'Up Jenkins', the hands would be raised, back of the hands facing across the table, and the others had to work out where the coin was hidden. They ordered various exercises – 'pianos' (make out you're playing a piano), 'windows' (wave your hands crosswise in the air), 'crabpots' (thump your fingers, up and down on the table), and finally, 'smashems' (crash your hands face down on the table, hard!). The hands were ordered up one by one, until the hand with the coin was the only one left, or that was the intention. Enormous glee when the opposition failed. Then the others had their go.

If we had visitors, the indoor games were different - Consequences, for instance, and blindfold games. Once, when there were a lot of people in the big sitting room at Winston, Tessy, blindfolded, was drawing people's names out of a hat and getting them to compose a letter to a person pre-nominated by her. Mrs Chappell was there, whose husband, Charlie, was our teacher, and reputed around the town to be an ardent left-winger. Mrs Chappell was given Joseph Stalin to write to. (I'm sure Tessy must have been peeping; she was capable of things like that!). At any rate, Mrs Chappell began, 'Dear Mr Stalin, my husband is very fond of you.' It brought the house down. We talked and laughed about it for years.

Occasionally we set up a kind of Ouija board – an upturned glass in the centre of the table - and all sat around it, everyone touching the glass. Tessy was usually the controller. We would put questions, and after a while the glass would start sliding towards one of the people or towards the place designated as 'Yes' or 'No'. It was totally out of our control, and returned amazing answers.

However, I wondered then and wonder to this day whether Tessy was in fact gently pushing that glass about, or perhaps all the others were in the know and hiding it from me.

Amazingly, we had only twenty books, or maybe a few more. I knew each one from cover to cover. There was a complete set of the Modern World Encyclopaedia. The last volume was the 'World Atlas'. I'd pore over this, playing games with myself, like fighting a war in the United States, moving my men around capturing this state, then the next, making tactical withdrawals at times, but always winning, naturally. 'Peril and Patriotism' consisted of epic tales of heroism throughout the Empire, with graphic drawings of scenes such as the death of General Gordon or, horror of horrors, a diver in the ocean depths, with his hand trapped in a giant clam. There was 'Robinson and Crusoe' to lift my imagination beyond my dull surroundings, and 'Swiss Family Robinson' as well. 'The Best of O Henry' was rather beyond my appreciation, but I read the stories just the same. The first one in the book, 'The Gift of the Magi', remains my all-time best short story ever, partly, I have to admit, because my mother was also greatly moved by it.

We children put together a magazine, called the 'Winston Journal' – stories, poems, and sketches by the four children, or that was the intention. I failed to have a single entry accepted by the editor, who must have been Tessy. That was no doubt because I didn't offer anything. I can't remember why. Probably because I was ashamed of having my inferior contribution permanently displayed to the world. I needn't have worried. Both editions of this publication have long since disappeared. Uncle Christopher, Mum's brother, sent a poem from Burma, where he was serving in the war. It was about a kangaroo/bounding through/the eucalyptus blue. Tessy, Angela and Noel were all excellent artists, and story-tellers, too. Tessy once made me a story-book about a cowboy and rustlers, written, illustrated, and sewn together by herself. This, too, has gone the way of all things.

I think the art, and possibly the music, that has turned out to be strong in the family further down the line, came from my father's Irish side, while the writing came from my mother. Dad's brother, John, a sad creature who was not able to care for himself throughout his life, nevertheless painted, using colours mixed from egg-yolks and other natural things. We never met John. Dad had little to do with any of his family.

On Christmas morning we woke up to a stocking full of presents at the end of our bed, an orange always at the bottom. After breakfast, our presents were opened. Mrs Pratt's parcel – something for each of us - was the most exciting. Something from Aunty Vivien would come through the post. Aunty Vivien lived in Melbourne. She wasn't a real aunt, but she had lived with Mum and her family in England in the really old days, so there was a special mystique about her. Often, she'd come on the train to visit us for the day, and her daughter, Daphne, just my age, sometimes came to stay. I was very fond of Daphne, and jealous, too, because she used to ride racehorses in trackwork at the Caulfield Racecourse, alongside all the famous jockeys whose names I knew so well.

Several times, when it was particularly hot at Christmas, Dick James would pick us all up and take us in the back of his utility to Picnic Pont at Longwarry North, where we would cavort in the Tarago River. One time he took us, perhaps just Noel and me, fishing in the Moe River. I must have been quite small because I remember thinking I was going to the Murray River!

We did have a real aunty – Aunty Janet. She was Mum's sister, and had come out from England soon after Mum did. Like Mum, she married out here and had four children, our first cousins, Noel, Rosalind, Margot, and Clem. Noel was about my age, the rest younger. Tom Mason – Uncle Tom – was the husband and father. He came and dug potatoes for us one time when Dad and Noel had grown a crop in the middle paddock. When Dad came to pay him, he threw the notes down on the ground. Dad picked them up and offered them to him once again. Again he threw them on the ground. I was standing alongside, and was awestruck by this exchange. Aunty Janet was a lovely, soft woman who later said and wrote very encouraging things to me, but there was an air of pathos about her, and she did have a hard life. I remember once staying by myself with the Masons when they were at St Albans in Melbourne, but we didn't have as much contact with our cousins as we might have had.

There were cousins on Dad's side, too, but we had hardly anything to do with them. On one occasion, Noel and I went to stay with an Aunt Maggie and her family up near Waubra, but just who exactly they were remained a mystery to my young understanding. A girl called Patricia

Ryan, who in some way was a cousin, came to stay with us later on. She embarrassed us all by wanting to go to Mass on Sunday morning, which posed a huge problem. How were we going to get her there? The Catholic Church was out on the Swamp, at Iona, three or four miles away. I can't remember how this was resolved. We probably found her a bike to ride. Sixty years afterwards, I tracked her down and got to know her well in her final years, at Ballarat. Later, Noel and I drove up to her funeral at Learmonth.

Chapter 6

To get to our place, you came up the track from the main road, past the pine plantation on one side and our old house, Lombardos', on the other, then through a gate, on to our land. That gate figured prominently in my life. It was one of those bush gates, made from boards and wire, and, like all such gates, swung badly from its hinges, so that it had to be lifted to be dragged open. When someone was leaving our place by car, say Mrs Pratt, Mum would send one of us children to open the gate for them, and as I was the youngest and got the most pleasure from it, I would race down the two hundred yards to open it, holding it open as they drove through. Occasionally, if someone was expected, I would go down and wait for them, holding the gate open so they could drive straight through. On Friday nights, I would keep a close watch on the gate, and when I saw Dad returning from work, I would run down and walk up the track with him, carrying his swag.

The other Friday night arrival was Mr Conlin's. The Conlins lived on a few acres next to us, and to get to their place they came through ours. Mr Conlin, like Dad, was away all week, working on a farm out on the Swamp, although he seemed so old I used to wonder how he could do it. On Friday nights, he arrived at our gate in his horse and jinker, and Noel and I would go tearing down to open up for him. He'd always have spent time at the pub before he arrived, and if we weren't there he would sit motionless, asleep, I think, until we came to open the gate for him. Then we'd walk beside him to open the next gate through to his place. Then came our reward. He'd produce a small white paper bag of lollies and as a pretended afterthought give us one each.

The Conlin family consisted of Mr and Mrs Conlin and Eily. Everybody said that Eily was not their daughter, but was really Eily Fallon, and had been brought up, perhaps adopted, by the Conlins. Mrs Conlin stayed at home all the time and looked after Sid. Sid was the most terrifying dog I've known in my life. He was a mangy grey/black and very large. He was tied up all the time and would bark and snarl ferociously, clawing at the ground and charging on his chain whenever anyone came near. If we had to go to the house, we had to go past Sid. Our hearts would almost fail as he thundered at us. Each time he charged we were sure the chain would break. He did get off one day, but we were safely at home, inside, at the time. We watched, as if from a bunker, as he ran around our place, dragging his broken chain. He seemed surprised and ill at ease. Like one of Plato's prisoners, he knew no other life than his kennel and chain. Mrs Conlin died of cancer. She just stayed at home and faded away. Her hair went white overnight, someone said. Mr Conlin lived on for a long time, until after we had left the place. One day he was found in our dam, drowned, poor old fellow. He must have gone down to check on something and slipped in.

Eily cut her hair short and wore overalls most of the time. Once, at a dance, we saw her in a dress. That was an amazing and incongruous sight. She worked on farms and orchards round about. Sometimes she'd be weeding carrots or else picking asparagus at Kinsella's; at other times she'd be packing apples at Parish's packing shed. She'd always get home just as we were having tea, and most nights would come in and stand just inside, leaning against the door, hands thrust into the shoulder straps of her overalls, muscles bulging on her forearms, her face burned by the sun. She would make jocular remarks about the apple pie we always seemed to be having. Often there'd be silences, or else Eily would just listen to the prattle and little rows that marked our evening meal. After a quarter of an hour, she would say goodbye and let herself out. We used to joke that Eily should have married Bill Parish, and she must have guessed what we were thinking because she was always throwing off at him. She did have a boy-friend towards the end of the War – Arthur Sharp was his name – and I remember him coming to visit her in his uniform, but it came to nothing. About that time a big company called Millers started up a linen thread factory in Warragul, though people always referred to it as the rope factory. It was the talk of the district, and quite a few people from Garfield went to work there. Eily was amongst them. I thought it was hardly right for someone like Eily to be working in a factory, nine to five, but I heard later, true or not, that she was looking after four machines, whereas everyone else looked after only one. Later she did marry and went to live in Warragul. I visited her once or twice, and she seemed happy, though out of place in her neat, double-fronted, brick veneer home.

Several times a year, we would climb Mount Cannibal, a low rocky prominence two or three miles from our place. The whole family might go, except for Dad, of course, or just two or three of us. Sometimes a team of visitors would be inveigled into coming. We'd walk up to the highway, and stay there for a while, playing games with the cars that came along. Three points for a car, two for a truck, and one for a motor-bike. Each vehicle 'belonged to' the next one of us in turn. Then we'd cross the highway and walk along the North Garfield road till we came to the power lines taking electricity from Yallourn to Melbourne. We'd stop and listen to the 'singing' of the wires, which we could hear by placing our ear against the metal towers. On to Cannibal Creek, where we'd look for fish, then on to the mountain itself. Through the side yard of the house at the foot of the mountain and straight up. No tracks in those times.

Our goal was always the Precipice, a large near-vertical rock face on the southern crest of the mountain. We'd scare our mother by climbing close to the edge. Angela would make up scary stories, like the man who dutifully looked after and faithfully guided his blind wife – that is, until the day he brought her here, held her arm, and said, 'Big step!' From there we could see to the Strzeleckis and the sea, though whether it was really the sea or just Noel and the others saying it was the sea, I could never be sure. One place I could be sure of was our own house there in the distance. If anyone was home, they'd wave a sheet at a time arranged beforehand. That was a huge thrill. My mother wrote a beautiful poem about Mount Cannibal:

> *Down on the Highway the traffic is lumbering,*
> *Milk trucks and motor cars rattle and race:*
> *Watching eternally, silent, unslumbering,*
> *Hoary old Cannibal stands in his place.*
>
> *There in that place that is his since Creation,*
> *Earthquakes have rocked him and meteors caressed:*
> *Who can interpret that grand contemplation?*
> *Or fathom the secrets he holds in his breast?*
>
> *Why must our years pass in grief and in sorrow?*
> *In haste and in ferment, in terror of death?*
> *Now is Infinity, now and tomorrow:*
> *There, on the mountain, is God's very breath.*

A lifetime later, when I began to write books for children, I wrote one about a disabled boy staying in the school camp in the old Garfield North School. He tries to climb Mount Cannibal despite his disability and a fierce storm that erupts. He sleeps in the cave that we used to explore, and gets to the Precipice, to look out over the vista we children used to look out at, overcoming the fears and doubts that had previously gripped him. One of the reviewers suggested there was more of myself in the story than I might like to admit!

Sometimes we would ride bikes to Mount Cannibal. Not always, because there were usually more walkers than bikes available. If there were two of us going a distance like to Bunyip or the Main Drain or Mount Cannibal, and we had only one bike, one would ride a hundred metres or so while the other set out walking. The first would leave the bike by the side of the road and walk on. The second would walk along, pick up the bike, ride past the now-walker, put down the bike, and go on. And so the miles were conquered. I remember feeling a comfortable sense of teamwork in the process. Another method of getting somewhere was to give a passenger a dink on the bar, if it was a boy's bike. But we didn't have much flesh on our bottoms at that age, and this wasn't a generally-favoured means of transport. Besides, it was hard work!

Just after we moved to 'Winston', I cut my bare foot on a piece of glass in the space between the house and the sleep-out one Saturday morning. It bled badly, and I had to get to the doctor's quickly. There was only one way to do I -: by bike. I got on Dad's back, piggy-back. He jumped on the one and only bike, which had no brakes. We had a hair-raising ride down the Garfield Hill, Dad putting his boot against the back tyre to stop us careering away to an early death. I had some stitches and was placed on crutches for several weeks. When he was putting the stitches in, Dr Paterson said I was as brave as a lion. I lapped it up!

When we moved from Lombardos' to Winston, I had just turned seven, so would have been in Grade three. Grade 3 were still with the littlies in the Little Room. Jocelyn Mauger had come as a new girl, so I had some tough competition. She was bright. I remember getting seventy-nine words correct in an eighty-word spelling test, but she got eighty! Nevertheless, it was I who was deputed to help Johnny Regnier with his work. He was placed next to me for this purpose, and he showed no indignation that he should be thus handed over to a fellow-student for tutoring. The Head Teacher, Mr Barrett, liked to have the whole school singing together. We'd all pack into the Middle

Room on Friday afternoons (there must have been a piano there), and shout the songs out. This was a strange and fascinating experience for me, especially when the big girls at the back started beefing it out in 'South of the Border,' one of the hits of the day:

> *South of the border, down Mexico way,*
> *That's where I fell in love*
> *When stars above came out to play.*
> *And now as I wander*
> *My thoughts ever stray*
> *South of the border, down Mexico way.*
>
> *Now she was a picture in old Spanish lace.*
> *Just for a tender while*
> *I kissed the smile upon her face,*
> *For it was Fiesta and we were so gay,*
> *South of the border, down Mexico way.*
>
> *Then she sighed as she whispered 'Manana',*
> *Never dreaming that we were to part,*
> *And I lied as I whispered 'Manana',*
> *For that tomorrow never came*

South of the border I rode back one day.
There in a veil of white,
By candlelight, she knelt to pray.
The bells there they told me that I mustn't stay
South of the border, down Mexico way

Ay ay ay ay, ay ay ay ay
Ay ay ay ay, ay ay ay ay

What a tangle of the uncertain elements of my young mind were gathered up there!

Each year the dentist's van would roll into the yard and park alongside the school building. We were called out by twos, alphabetically. We dreaded it and returned either with grins of relief or with hands held to our swollen cheeks. Ronnie Cox and I were called together one year. I remember because the dentist came into the room with his list and said, no doubt in an attempt to lighten the general mood, "Next, Jim Tim Connelly and Connie Rox." There was no dentist in town, although every now and then a man would come and set up his chair in the Supper Room at the

Hall on Saturdays. I don't believe he did anything except extractions.

I'm not sure at what level we began to have exams, but it was probably in Grade 4. I had a fear of exams because I had heard fearsome accounts of them from Tessy and Angela at High School. We were horribly superstitious in those times. We firmly believed that "a piece of glass will make you pass", and we wouldn't have dreamed of going in to an exam without a shard of broken glass in our pocket. One day, on the morning of an exam, one of the big kids, Alan Goldsack, spoke kindly to me, telling me not to worry and that things would go well. I was powerfully struck by this, no doubt because encouragement was something hardly known to me.

On Monday mornings, the whole school – seventy or eighty of us – lined up in our classes on the gravel area beside the school to salute the flag. The Head Teacher would raise the flag, we would place our hands on our hearts, and repeat the words of the prescribed oath of allegiance. This went, *'I promise to love God and my country, to serve the King, honour the flag, and cheerfully obey my parents, teachers, and the laws'*. Frankie Grant, who lived out on the Thirteen Mile Road, was late to school every Monday morning, arriving soon after the Oath ceremony was over. He belonged to a curious religious sect. This strong appeal to loyalty, to the established order of things, was backed up by the School Readers, Grade 1 to Grade 8. Over the years I've managed to collect the whole set from Op Shops and second-hand bookshops. These readers were issued to all students at the beginning of each year, and contained a heavy dose of Australian stories and poems, especially of the bush. I'll quote one of these, partly because I learnt it in Grade 4 and it has been in my mind down through the years. I see through its crude sentiment and its banal simplicities, but it's tucked itself into my heart, perhaps because it's a reminder of the old and simpler order of things. It meshed, as well, with my emerging religious sense.

OVER THE RANGE (Banjo Paterson)

"Little bush maiden, wondering-eyed,
Playing alone in the creek bed dry,
In the small green flat on every side
Walled in by the Moonbi Ranges high.
Tell us the tale of your lonely life

Mid the great grey forests that know no change."
"I never have left my home," she said.
"I have never been over the Moonbi Range."

"Father and Mother are both long dead
And I live with Granny in yon wee place."
"Where are your father and mother?" we said.
She puzzled a while with a thoughtful face;
Then a light came into the shy, brown eye,
And she smiled, for she thought the question strange
On a thing so certain – "When people die,
They go to the country over the range."

"And what is this country like, my lass?"
"There are blossoming trees and pretty flowers,
And shining creeks where the golden grass
Is fresh and sweet from the summer showers.
They never need work, nor want, nor weep;
No troubles can come their hearts to estrange.
Some summer night I shall fall asleep,
And wake in the country over the range."

"Child, you are wise in your simple trust,
For the wisest man knows no more than you.
Ashes to ashes, dust to dust;
Our views by a range are bounded, too;
But we know that God hath this gift in store,
That, when we come to the final change,
We shall meet with our loved ones gone before
To the beautiful country over the range."

By the time I got to the Big Room, Mr Chappell had arrived as Head Teacher. He was very interested in the environment and had us growing vegetables and planting trees. The Chappells became quite good friends. Norma Chappell was the same age as Angela. Mr Chappell was captain of the cricket team, so came in for detailed criticism of his performance from Dad, especially after Noel started playing. I don't know why Mr Chappell should have taken so much interest in Noel and me, but he was very good to us, sometimes taking us away with his family to holidays at Queenscliff during the holidays. I was mad on cricket at this time, and used to play imaginary games with imaginary teams. I remember doing this down at Queenscliff during one of these holidays. One of my imagined players I named

'Warne', but he wasn't a leg spinner; he was a wise old stager.

The school provided treats for us every now and then. I remember a sports meeting with other schools, though people complained because we were given purple colours to compete in instead of Garfield's gold and green. I have stronger memories of the annual beach picnic. The whole school would cram into the back of a truck. Tarpaulins were stretched over the metal framework to stop us being blown off. There were benches around the sides for the big kids and the little ones sat on the floor. We could see nothing at all on the journey, but then we would step out at Edithvale to the sunshine and the sparkling water. I'd return home sunburnt all over!

Each year a dark cloud descended over the whole school. This was the visit of the School Inspector. For weeks before his arrival, the teacher would threaten and bully us with tales of how he would deal with us if our work and manners and dress were found to be unsatisfactory. Then, the terrible day of his arrival came. His big black car pulled up at the front of the school. His ominous shape appeared through the glass of the classroom door. He was introduced. "Good morning, children." "Good morning, Mr Curtis." For two days he went through our books and questioned us on the work we had been doing. Little did we think that he was no doubt going through the teacher's books after we had gone for the day, and questioning him, also. There was a first day, then a second day, then he was gone, like winter, the wearisome guest, in Henry Kendall's poem, and we all breathed more easily.

The war affected our school lives. We spent time on Friday afternoons making camouflage nets and brought money for War Saving certificates on Tuesday mornings. Each sixpence was rewarded with a stamp. The stamps were pasted into a card with thirty-two spaces. So each completed card was worth sixteen shillings. After the war the card could be redeemed for one pound, twenty shillings.

Together with the rest of the Garfield community, we raised money for an Army ambulance. It was brought down from Melbourne and parked in the main street. Everyone came to admire it. The new vegetable garden at school was part of the war effort. We didn't dig air raid shelters at school, but Noel and I mattocked out a small one at home. We had fears the Japanese pilots would mistake our poultry sheds for a factory and we would all be blown to smithereens. Les James, Noel's friend, put the idea into our heads. We had ration cards for a lot of our everyday items – meat, butter, tea, sugar, and clothing. Petrol was rationed, too, but it mattered not to us. We had no car.

However, the war was a constant presence in the life of the town. We had to brown-out our windows at night, and car headlights were hooded. Because of the shortage of petrol, many cars had gas-producers set up on their running boards, burning charcoal to produce gas to fire the engine. All the road signs were taken down. This caused a good deal of amusement; we'd laugh at the idea that though the Japanese might be clever enough to invade Gippsland, they wouldn't be clever enough to find their way to Melbourne without the road signs. It was always surprising to see men we knew well from around town appearing in Army uniform overnight. Actually, Dad went down to Melbourne to join up, but he was forty-nine at the time, and he failed the medical exam. I remember him coming home after returning on the train quite late at night, with all of us sitting up, waiting to hear if he would be going to war.

One of my classmate's brothers, Ivan Leask, was killed in New Guinea. He and his best mate, Roy Hunter from Drouin, died together. There was a beautiful notice put in the paper: "Side by side they fought through heat and wind and hail; now side by side they sleep along the Kokoda Trail". We poked fun at Hitler and Mussolini. At a fancy-dress event in the Hall, I went as Rudolf Hess, the Nazi Cabinet Minister who had just parachuted into Scotland. I can't remember what Mum got me to wear, but I had a black umbrella for a parachute, with a swastika in cut-out paper pasted on the front.

It was about this time – when the war was felt to be putting us in danger – that Robert Nutting came to live with us for six months. The Nuttings were friends. Don, the oldest of the children, used to help with showing the pictures on Saturday nights, Beth was Tessy's special friend, and Robert was my age or a little bit younger. The Nuttings by this time had moved to Melbourne. We boarded up one of the open front verandas for Bobby to sleep in. I don't think he was very happy while with us, especially after he shot Tessy in the leg with his air rifle. I came along one day to find Tessy lying on the sofa, writhing in pain. That in itself was an amazing thing, Tessy being such a stoic. Somehow, the air rifle had gone off, the pellet hitting Tessy in the leg, and Bobby had cleared off down the bush in panic. The wound was superficial, and all was resolved without too much drama.

After Bobby had gone back to Melbourne, I moved out of the sleep-out and into his room, to my immense pleasure. The only problem with my new accommodation was that there were large spaces between the floorboards, and every rustle in the night meant a black snake twisting itself towards me and into my bed. There were myriad stories going the rounds in the schoolyard about snakes getting into people's beds. It happened to Stan Styles, everybody knew!

Many people who write about their upbringing tell how there was fierce feeling between Catholics and Protestants in the 'thirties and 'forties. I must begin a revisionist movement here. I was aware that there were Catholics and they were somehow different from us, but I never saw any overt inter-church hostility at the State School. The fact that Dad came from a Catholic family and that I had Catholic relations passed entirely over my head. During the war, there was feeling amongst us about Germans, which I now deeply regret. The two Schmutter brothers, Ken and Ted, came in for some nasty abuse, once, I'm sad to say, from me. Poor fellows. I'm not sure they were even aware of their family's German origin. They were as Australian as any of us.

Some children at school went on to Grade 8, by which time they would be fourteen and able to leave school. The alternative was to leave at the end of Grade 6 and go to Warragul High School. In my year, only Mavis Johnson and I went on to High School. That entailed an entrance exam, though I think it was more of a grading exercise by the High School. The entrance exam was at the Bunyip school, so the two of us rode bikes there for the big event. Visiting another school was almost unknown. I can remember going to another school only one other time, and that was when we were very small – in Grade 1 or 2 – and had a football game against the Iona Convent School. We were so ignorant of the game we deliberately kicked points so the ball would stay at our end of the ground! Later, years later, I started to dream of being an Australian test cricketer and an Essendon footballer! Maybe it was time for me to move on to High School.

Chapter 7

I'm not sure, really, I *was* ready for High School. I had to be rescued on my first day. I was desperate to be placed in Lyall House, Tessy's house. She left school and started at Uni just as I began at Warragul High. Angela and Noel were in Haines. That first day, they put me in Swinburne – Swinburne! That most despised collection of under-beings! A craven note from my mother the next day put things right, but I was off to a bad start. It was 1944 and I was barely ten and a half. Nowadays, I meet little children in Grade 5, still playing with their teddy-bears and dolls houses, and I find they're ten and a half. Did I miss out on childhood, or was I too young to mix it in the rough world of secondary education? Tick both boxes.

We were issued with a Report Book as soon as we arrived. It stayed with us for all our six years. I've still got it! Every mark and every subject report was entered therein. In no way could we put behind us the shameful record of earlier years. Besides, in writing my name on the dotted line on page one, I blotted the ink. The blot and my childish hand are still there to mock me all these years later. The Report

Book was the same one issued to all secondary students in the State. 'It should prove of great value to the pupil', it says in the front, 'and is the best testimonial which can be given for future use'. Well, here's my testimonial for Term 1, 1944. English 74%, French 74%, Maths 75%, Science 62%, Geography 61%, History 81%, Drawing P. Number in Form 44. Place in Form 8th. 'A keen and interested student. Pleasing results', said Miss Emms, the Form Teacher. Next term I was fourth. The next twelfth. The reports changed. 'Could do better'. 'Not working to the best of his ability'. 'Too great a tendency to do just as much as is absolutely necessary.' Did they know I was busting my boiler to do well? That I was spending three hours a day on the school bus? That I was leaving home before the sun was up and getting home in the gathering gloom? That all my homework was done by the light of candles or kerosene lamp? Ah, poor me! I can always find my way to some excuse! Tessy had been Dux of the School the year before, suffering under the same difficulties!

I have a book with every student's name in it, in Form order, from 1911 to 1986. It's one of my most used resources. There were 132 of us starting in Form 1 that year, 1944. Looking through the list now, I can remember to the point of visualising them more than fifty, while most of the other names ring a bell of some kind. Some, like Norm Henry, Graeme Smethurst, Bill Dryden, George Colson, Bill Malloy, and Ian Torbet, were in my Form most or all of the way through school. My best friend was Jim Willis. His father had been almost completely deafened by an exploding shell in the First World War. I sometimes went to stay with the Willises on their farm in Hazeldean Road, south of Yarragon, and Jim came to stay at our place. Jim was born with a cleft palate so it was hard to understand him until one became used to his speech. He lived a lonely life, unmarried, working with the State Electricity Commission at Yallourn, and becoming well-known as a boundary umpire for the Yarragon football team. He used to run the roads around the district for miles and miles. Athletics was his one abiding interest. We continued in intermittent contact over the years, and in 1999, I conducted his graveside funeral service in the Warragul cemetery.

A couple of years before my arrival, Mr Baker, the Senior Master, and Miss Styles, the Senior Mistress, had combined to write the School Song. I took its final verse very seriously:

To Warragul High School, the pride of West Gippsland,

The centre of learning, the School on the Hill,

Ringed in by the mountains, Strzelecki and Baw Baw,

We come from the farmland, the township, the mill.

From Drouin, Trafalgar, Poowong, and Longwarry,

From Yarragon, Garfield, Nayook, and Seaview,

From Neerim and Lardner and Bunyip and Noojee,

In buses, on cycles, our ways we pursue.

So here's to the school of our youth and our dreaming;

Through life's changing fortunes, we'll honour her still.

In lessons, in study, in sport, and in leisure,

We pledge our life's best to the School on the Hill.

The teachers at school were friendly, but not overly helpful nor encouraging. Miss Dudley, who took us for History in Form 5, showed some interest in me, and Mr Lacy, in Form 6 History, to some extent, but for the others, we were just a class, not individuals with varying needs and capabilities.

There was a good deal of copying from notes on the blackboard or notes dictated to us. In the senior classes, we'd read communally from a text-book, pausing for some explanations or some discussion as we did.

Because of a dire shortage of space, our classes in Form 6 were held in odd places – the Principal's office, the Staff Room, and the front veranda of the main building. Miss Marrabel took us for English in Form 4. She was short and plump, and sat on the teachers' desk, from where she could kick misbehavers in the front seat, including me on one occasion. Mr Greenwell was young and glamorous. I remember him taking us for Science in Form 3 and giving me glimpses of a world beyond my ken. Mr Tozer was also young and glamorous. He was a top-class cricketer who later played for the State. He was one of the staff members I came close to when I became Captain of Cricket in my final year. Mr Hallett was a cynical man-of-the-world who taught us French. He told us one day he'd received a letter from someone he knew in France who'd written about the American band leader, 'Du Kellington'! Miss Worthington was also young and attractive, and most of us boys aspired to be in love with her. Many years later she re-entered my life, for she married and remained in the district.

The School Principal throughout my time was Dr Harris – William John Harris. We respected him greatly, but had no idea of his personal background – that he was a notable geologist, who in collaboration with a man from the Department of Mines had done amazing work in the field here in Victoria. The two of them were responsible for a revised scheme for the classification of graptolites which has been followed throughout most of the world. The Australian Dictionary of Biography describes him as "one of the most significant palaeontologists and stratigraphers of the twentieth century". Nor did we know that just before coming to Warragul from ten years as Principal of Echuca High School he had lost both his wife and his son. Happily he married again and remained at the school for two years after I had left.

Every now and then, a Social was held at school. These were at night, so problems arose about getting home afterwards. One of these must have been when I was in Form 3. The Athlone bus stayed to take kids home at the end of the evening, so I arranged to stay with Graeme Smethurst who lived at Athlone. I remember being embarrassed with some of the games. In one, everyone had to take off their shoes, which were put in a great pile at the opposite side of the hall. We were all paired up, into girl-boy couples. There was a race to find one's shoes, put them on and present to the judges' box as a properly shoed couple. The embarrassment came because of the shoddy nature of my footwear and the even shoddier state of my socks which thus were unveiled, without warning. The authorities should have been more understanding of us country kids! On the way home, there was some furtive pairing off at the back of the bus. I was emboldened to slide alongside one particular girl and sat with my arm around her for the duration of the journey. She was at least compliant. Fifty years later, when I came back to West Gippsland, we came across each other, frequently. Neither of us ever gave the slightest flicker of recognition of that far-off night of adolescent experiment.

One of the features of school life at High School were the school parades. Once every couple of months the whole school formed into House groups on the school oval, in a square, Colvin, Haines, Lyall, and Swinburne, each House in three ranks. First came the inspection. The official party consisting of the Senior Master and Mistress and one or two other staff members, moved around the assembled House groups examining shoes, clothing, hair, and even fingernails, offering reproofs to offending students, while assiduously making notes and entering scores in their notepads all the while. We stood stiffly to attention while this was happening. Then the marching began. A bass drum and a couple of kettle drums banged away and we all marched around and around, again being closely examined. All this was taken deadly seriously, by me, at any rate. I wouldn't have moved a muscle during the whole performance. At the end, the points were announced and the winner declared, while the House Captains would extol their charges to do better next time.

There was no indoor assembly room at the school. Each week we assembled at the rear of the school in Form groups, the girls on the lower level and the boys on the asphalt playing area above the steps. Members of staff would make announcements about various activities, then the Senior Master and Mistress would speak of disciplinary matters, then Dr Harris would speak more generally about the tone of the school and such things. I can remember only one thing he ever said, and that was that no one new to Warragul wishing to visit the school would have any trouble finding it. All they needed to do was follow the trail of litter from the town centre and they'd arrive at the school. He wasn't usually so sarcastic.

Chapter 8

I learnt in these years that I wasn't cut out to be a law-breaker. My semi-criminal experiences were always accompanied by the most intense feelings of guilt. I'd found that out earlier, in State School. One day, Noel and I walked into Whelan's sweet shop. We knew they always stayed in their own place at the back until they heard the tinkle of the bell that sounded whenever someone entered, then emerged, usually quite slowly. They kept a glass jar filled with snowballs on the counter, and Noel assured me that if we went in and snatched a couple of snowballs, we would be clear of the place before the Whelans emerged. We succeeded, but as we walked away, Mr Whelan opened the door into the street and said, 'Did you boys want something?' 'No,' Noel replied, innocently, over his shoulder, and we walked away. My guilt stayed with me for a long time.

However, that was nothing compared with my Great Train Fraud. I'd stayed back at High School for football training, and caught the train home to Garfield afterwards, when it was quite dark. Some tempter had whispered in my ear that if you slid on board when no one was looking and got off on the wrong side of the train at your destination, you could thus travel without a ticket. I did it. My heart was in my mouth all the way, and when I jumped off on the side opposite the platform and hid behind a goods shed until Mr Graham had returned to the station office, then slinked off up the hill and to home, I suffered all the tortures of the damned.

At home I joined the scout troop when it was re-established by Bill Parish after being in recession for some years. I became Troop Leader, and had a silver badge at the front of my scout hat to show my rank. I even became a First Class Scout. However, I was rather hopeless at tying knots or lashing poles together. I've found in life that if you don't know how to do something and stand around looking interested, someone will eventually appear who can do what needs to be done. I've applied this principle consistently throughout my adult life, notably when I was a sergeant during National Service and also during my twelve years as a scoutmaster at Cranbrook in Sydney.

Most of the boys of my age in Garfield were scouts. We'd sometimes go out to the scout camp site on Cannibal Creek in North Garfield, where Bill, who was very knowledgeable about such things, would point out the old Cobb and Co coach route, where it crossed the creek. We could even see the foundations of the bridge that took the road across the creek. Every Easter we'd go to a big camp at Gilwell Park in Gembrook, riding in the back of Bill's utility. On Friday nights we had our parades in the Garfield Hall, where Bill and Fred Cox, the Assistant Scoutmaster, drilled us. Afterwards the boys gathered under the shelter of the Baby Health Centre alongside, exchanged dirty stories, and smoked cigarettes. Not me, of course.

When I was fifteen and in Form 5, in what must have been my last year as a scout, I went to a camp for Senior Scouts on Fraser Island in Queensland. The Victorian contingent travelled over three hellish days by train to get there. I'd made myself, with Bill Parish's and my mother's help, a Queensland bell tent, as recommended, with instructions, in the scout journal. The oil I used to waterproof it soaked into all my things, so I spent a very messy three weeks in camp. Instead of a back-pack, I took my gear in a swagman's roll, also as recommended. When I got to the camp, I found I was the only one of the many hundreds who had either a bell tent or a swagman's roll. The rest – clever city types, mostly - had back-packs and smart modern one-man tents! Live and learn? It doesn't seem to be my style.

Smoking was very common in those days. It wasn't just the done thing; it was the glamorous thing to do. The film stars all smoked. The ideal of a beautiful woman was a tall, shapely blonde leaning on a veranda rail in southern USA, languidly drawing on a cigarette. All of us young fellows – I'm sure it wasn't just me – pictured ourselves growing into that young-man-about-town scene where we would casually produce our cigarette, light it in a cupped hand, put it to our lips with a grizzled frown on our foreheads, and mutter some clever remark to the admiring group gathered around us.

This is all leading up to the Great Lang Lang Rodeo Adventure. The Lang Lang Rodeo was held on Easter Monday each year. It was celebrated all over West Gippsland. A bus ran there for the day from Garfield, and one year, when I was probably thirteen or fourteen, I went on this bus. Once arrived, I took a ticket on the spinning jenny, and won! 'Choose your prize,' the man said. I looked at the dazzling array of gifts mounted there, but I had eyes for only one – six blue ten-packs of Capstan cigarettes. Nobody I knew was around. I pointed to the cigarettes. In a moment they were mine! At home, I had a problem. The solution was to stash the forbidden fruit amongst the hay in the loft above shed number 7, and every time there was nobody at home over the next couple of months I would get up there and puff away amidst my delusions of grandeur. I couldn't manage the draw-back; I would draw the smoke in and immediately puff it out again. That probably saved my lungs from savage disrepair. What I did with the butts and how I covered the resulting smell of smoking I can't remember. But I got away with it completely. Oddly enough, a couple of years later I met a boy from my old grade, Ray Petty, who had left school by then. He lit up a cigarette in the main street of Garfield – the main street of Garfield, with lots of people around! I was shocked to the core.

The Garfield Hall had many associations for us. Perhaps twice each year, a concert was got up, where various local people would perform, including members of our family. I remember Ian Costain, later to be brother to my brother-in-law, with his guitar and singing in a pleasant voice to his own accompaniment. Mrs Bassed might play a piano solo, while Dorothy Bassed would sing some song like 'Cherry

Ripe' or 'Comin' through the Rye' in her lovely soprano voice.

There was an old stager called Bumper Gee, who was renowned far and wide for his comedy turns and tall tales. He was there one night on one of his last appearances because he was even then an old man, I remember. I was waiting in the supper room for my act, whatever it was that night, when Bumper rushed up – he had already been announced –pushed past me, saying, 'What can I do? What can I do?' He saw the supper laid out, grabbed a half-sandwich and went on stage playing the sandwich as though it were a mouth organ. He brought the house down, as always. It was Bumper Gee who told me that the Bunyip Fire Engine had once sunk under the surface in the old days when the Swamp was still a swamp, and remains there to this day. I've never met anyone to corroborate that tale, but I'm convinced it's true and that the Fire Engine will one day be found by a puzzled farmer, vindicating both Bumper Gee and myself.

I played cameo parts in various concert performances. Towards the end of the war, someone got together an item where a group from the school sang the Andrews Sisters song, 'Three Little Sisters.' The chorus was 'One loved a soldier, one loved a sailor, and one loved a lad from the marines.' Three of us small boys were dressed up, and every time the chorus came round, we'd step forward in turn and sing our line in our high squeaky voices, in my case '... and one loved a lad from the marines'. I couldn't sing then and I can't sing now! We used to act in plays at these concerts, we Connellys. Mum often used to write the plays herself, and was the producer, and director as well. We children all took part. In one of them, I was a crystal-gazer, and Tessy a woman who came to see me. The only other play I can remember was not one of my mother's, but out of a book. It was called 'The Bathroom Door', and Tessy and I, then probably nineteen and thirteen, were the main, probably the only, players. The action took place outside a closed bathroom door, while we waited for our turn to use it. It was empty all the time, of course, but the waiting and the discussion had changed our lives in ways I can't recall. [STOP PRESS. I've just googled 'The Bathroom Door' and found the following precis. I submit it as testimony to the fallibility of memory:

A prima donna, a young man, an old man, an old lady, and a young lady are all trying to get into a bathroom in a hotel in this one act comedy. The door will not open, and at last the prima donna declares that her husband with whom she has had a quarrel must have locked himself in the bathroom and done away with himself. Enter then a servant who discloses the fact that the door is not locked at all, and the bathroom is empty.]

In my second year in High School, Mum's Aunt Anna in England died. She and Mum had kept in touch over the years. Still, it was an amazing surprise to us, but maybe not to Mum, that she left £4,000 to my mother. That's the figure I've always carried in my head, though, on reflection, it seems too extraordinarily large. Maybe part of it went to pay off the house. The rest was used to build two large bedrooms – dormitories, we called them – and an attached bathroom alongside the house. Mum had always dreamed of having a holiday home for children. Now she could realise her dream. But, as always, we proved to be a divided family over the matter. To Dad it was a crazy scheme. The older children were at best lacklustre about the idea. Sensing my mother needed some comfort, I sided strongly with her. That's the way things generally went in the Connelly family!

Mum resisted the doubters and went ahead. Dick James and his brother-in-law, Charlie Rowlerson, did the work, and the children started to arrive. Mum must have put an advertisement in one of the Melbourne papers. They were good middle-class children, some brothers and sisters, and a few came back many times in school holidays. All were from Melbourne, except for Dr Martin's children from Garfield. Mum fussed over them like a character in a children's book of Victorian times. Some of them, and their parents, said kind things and Mum got a lot of pleasure from the venture, despite the fact that the numbers remained very small. I've recently come across a notebook where I wrote down some of their names: "Staying at home for the school holidays are Ross Snow (4), Laurence Bear (10), Dennis Martin (5), Vivian Martin (10) and another one expected – Tony Guttmann". Financially, it was a total failure.

Mum was always on the look-out for people who needed a helping hand. So it was that she answered an advertisement in one of the women's journals from 'Desperate' who needed short-term accommodation for herself and her small son. She arrived on the train and was set up in one of the dormitories. We soon realised that we had come across someone very different from anyone we had yet encountered in our sheltered lives. The first realisation came on her second day, when, into the general conversation, she dropped the question of whether we knew how a cat could lift a bottle of beer from the floor on to the table. We were stunned enough by the question, but the answer completely floored us. You wrap a towel around the bottle of beer, place the cat on the towel and pick it up by its tail. The cat will dig its claws hard into the towel and thus lift the beer on to the table top. The lady stayed for five or six uncomfortable weeks, until, as she was making no discernible efforts to find some other place to live, Mum asked her to go.

My mother was widely recognised as something of a ministering angel. At her death years later, an obituary in the local paper, said, "She will be remembered for her capacity to befriend people, and in particular those in need of help or reassurance." One family she befriended were the Sturdys. In fact, we all seemed to spend a lot of time with them. Tessy had stayed there for the six weeks Mum was away in hospital, for instance. George Sturdy lived up to his name. He was a big, barrel-chested, genial man from the English West Country. He had quite a large apple orchard, but worked away from home during the week as a ganger on the railways. His wife, Belle, was very different.

She conducted a lively social life in the town. There were seven children, all boys. (Garfield was noted at that time for large families of boys. There were the Paynes who played football, the Sturdys, and the Millers, again seven boys, one of whom, 'Frosty' Miller, became a famous footballer in Melbourne). The older Sturdy boys were about our age. They were often at our place, and we'd visit them, walking through the bush at the back of our place to get there. Belle Sturdy's maiden name must have been Geoghegan. There were often male relations of hers there by that name, sometimes drinking beer and playing the guitar. One of them once told me he had been 'in quod' and had to explain what that meant. I was immediately in awe of him. Mum tried to keep the Sturdy boys on the straight and narrow. I think I'm right in saying that she arranged to have the children baptised and was godmother to them. I do remember that the whole family respected Mum deeply.

The time came when Noel started to play first cricket and then football for Garfield. Dad and I would go to the games and watch in a pitch of excitement. Dad would fume and silently swear when injustices were done to Noel, like not being given a bowl when we were losing the match, or some football opponent giving him a hard time. For cricket, we would travel to away games in Keith Sarah's car or perhaps Mr Chappell's. Sometimes I rode my bike. Once I set off to ride to Nar Nar Goon, but one of the team cars overtook me and gave me a lift. I hid my bike under a bridge and collected it on the way back. On one occasion, Lindsay Hassett and Ian Johnson, both famous Test cricketers, were speaking at the Cora Lynn Hall in the off-season. I rode my bike there and back again, without a light, across the pitch-black roads of the Swamp. I was mad for cricket! Hassett told a story of the first time he was picked to play for Australia. He was listening in a hotel bar as the team for England was read out over the radio. The announcer began, 'Bradman, Barnes, Badcock, Brown, Barnett …', and Hassett turned to his drinking mate and said, "How am I ever going to get in the team with all those 'B's in it?!"

I was obsessed with football and cricket. As soon as we arrived at High School we would be kicking the football on the frozen grass of the oval. In summer, we'd be playing cricket, on the oval again, every break and lunchtime. At home it was the same. Noel and I would play kick to kick in winter, while in summer, we'd set up some stumps in the front paddock on the smoothest piece of ground we could find and take it in turns to bat and bowl. This led to continued arguments about who should fetch the ball when it was hit into undefined fielding territory. I always lost the argument! But I didn't need Noel to play football. I played on my own for hours. Noel, who spent Forms 3 and 4 at Caulfield Tech before returning to Warragul High, brought back from Caulfield the brilliant invention of the boys' woodwork aprons being rolled and tied up tightly and used as footballs. The backyard near the feed shed was my football ground and one of these aprons was my football. The space between the corner of the feed shed and a big gum tree was the goal. I'd take towering high marks, spin and twist, fend off imaginary opponents, bounce the ball, and kick magnificent goals with either foot to give Essendon another close victory. Then do it all over again ... and again! I was the greatest!

I played my first game of cricket for Garfield – there were no Seconds or junior teams then – when I was twelve or thirteen. They put me in at number 11, and I steadily worked my way up the order, one place at a time, until I was opening the batting a couple of years later. Noel was a very good fast bowler and good bat; I was more a batsman. In football, it was much the same. Noel was an established player when I began. I was in Form 6, so at the start of the season I would have been fifteen. I was 19th man for the first seven games and didn't get on to the field. In those days, the 19th man went on the field only if another player came off, not allowed to return for the rest of the match. At last I was picked in the team proper. Five minutes after the match started, I was going for the ball near our goal when the umpire's whistle went. I looked around in surprise. "In the back", he was saying and pointing to me. I took the ball and steered it through the posts with my first kick!

In football, Pakenham were our major opponents. In my second season we played a draw against them in the Preliminary Final, then lost the re-play by ten goals. There were a lot of hardened men in our team, the 'Garfield Stars'. I remember them all, but a few of them have stuck particularly in my mind. Frank Kennedy, strong as an ox, was our coach in my first year. He had played VFL for Melbourne. Mick O'Hehir was a tough half-back who played as if it was Armageddon. Ken Duncan was a magnificent mark and kick. Everyone said he should have played League. Pinky Dryden played rover and forward pocket and used to kick clever left-foot goals. He did best when he'd had a skinful at the pub that morning. Clem Pitt was full back, and would reach the centre when kicking out. Stan Edis was very fast – he competed in professional foot-running – with a terrific stab-kick. Then there were the Paynes – four brothers, all big tough men. Pat, the oldest, retired at the end of each year, but, next season, he would hear the football being kicked down at the ground from where he lived. He couldn't resist it and came back and played again.

When I began I felt strongly that I was a boy amongst men. I recall very little about individual games, but I remember the little thrill I got when the great Frank Kennedy hand-balled to me in my first game. He trusted me! One shock came when at three-quarter time in a home game on a bitterly cold day and we were behind, someone passed a bottle of sherry around the huddle. 'Get some steam into you,' they said. I declined!

In cricket, our bete-noire was Cora Lynn, where Ian and Ewen Costain played. We won one premiership against them in very dubious circumstances. We batted first, and they were one run behind us with the last two men in. I was fielding at mid-off and noticed some dark goings-on between one of our fieldsmen and the bowler, Freddy Russell. The latter then ran in to bowl, brought his arm over, but retained the ball. Ewen, who was at the non-striker's end, dashed for the other end. Meanwhile Freddy took the bails off, and Ewen was run out. It was a dirty deed, but we had won by one run. Ewen, maddened beyond control, took after Freddy with his bat, chasing him all over the field until he was subdued.

Cricket was a 'dry' game. There was a polite afternoon tea for both teams served by the home ladies half way through the day's play. Nobody from the team ever went to the pub after the game, but football was quite different. Just about the whole team would adjourn there after a home match, excepting the ones who had to get home to milk. The pub was a hostile and dangerous place to me, and I would walk with Dad straight home after a game. None of the others expected me to join them, and, anyhow, I was under age.

There was never any drink in our home. Not a drop! So it came as a violent shock to me, many years later, when I was in middle age, to learn from the others that Dad had in fact once been a heavy drinker. He must have given it up, cold-turkey, as they say, soon after I was born. I had my first drop of the demon drink at an Army camp when I was doing National service, aged eighteen, in less than salubrious circumstances. Someone had managed to smuggle in some beer, and I had a taste from a tin pannikin in one of the huts after lights out, in the deep dark. By then, of course, I had forsworn the pledge I'd signed four or five years earlier as a piece of deceitful manipulation of a defenceless child!

I had no idea about my future career. Tessy had gone on to do Science at university; Angela went from school to Teachers College, and Noel left school after Form 5 to go into surveying. Mum had ideas about me being a lawyer. It was the time-honoured career of her family, the Hazards, and for two years I did Latin by correspondence in preparation for the law. But that idea petered out. When I was thirteen, Mum, again, enthused me about joining the Navy through their Officer Cadet intake of boys of that age. Accordingly, I applied, and passed the academic entrance exam. However they failed me on unspecified medical grounds. Seven hundred applied; sixteen were chosen. I wasn't disappointed. A close friend of mine at school, Graeme Smethurst, applied as I did, and also failed the medical. He was, however, unlike me, really keen on having a career at sea, and went off after Form 5 to train as a merchant seaman. He became a Master Mariner and has spent his life in charge of big ships and, more recently, instructing others at a maritime Training College.

Going to university was the natural thing to do after Form 6, but we couldn't afford the fees. I would have to win a Commonwealth Scholarship, as Tessy had done, or else apply for a Studentship to be trained as a Secondary School teacher, where my fees would be paid and I would receive a small living allowance, in exchange for being bonded to teach for the Education Department for three years. This is what happened. After my matriculation year I drifted into university and consequently into teaching.

There was an obstacle, however. I was too young to be accepted at university. Seventeen was the minimum age, and I was sixteen years and four months when I matriculated at the end of 1949. Tessy had also been under age, but escaped this restriction because the age was lowered to sixteen during the war years. I've forgotten if I considered any other options for that gap year, but the easiest thing was to become a Student Teacher. This I did, and was appointed to Garfield State School. The older children were not a great deal younger than myself, though that didn't really matter because I was given Grade 4 for most of the time. The Head Teacher was Mr Fischer, who by then had succeeded our friend, Mr Chappell. We got along quite well. I was useful to him. On one occasion he got me to go to a parent's home to complain about their dog following the children to school, which task I was ill-equipped to do. On another occasion, he got me to climb a swaying thirty-foot ladder, most precariously, to gain access to the loft in the main classroom, a task he thought I might be better at than him! There was a Student Teachers training camp at Queenscliff half way through the year. It was the first time I had mixed with a group of others of about my own age in such a way, and was a good preparation for university, I can see now.

It was about then – probably during my year as a student teacher – that Mum bought a car. This was an unexpected and extraordinary thing, but then Mum liked to surprise people. It was second-hand, a little light green car, a Ford Anglia, I think. It had a canvas hood, which presumably could have been taken down, but never was. Mum had previously sometimes ridden a bicycle when she didn't walk into town. But now, licence in handbag, she would beetle carefree about the countryside. The number-plate was SD 344. Dad never drove, but he would sometimes ride in it, with Mum at the wheel, though I can imagine his feelings when he did so. I got my driver's licence in it. Mr Pringle, the policeman, watched me drive a few hundred yards along the main street, turn around and come back again. He'd seen me driving before this, of course. The car never seemed to break down, and Mum kept it happily until she and Dad moved to Melbourne some years later.

Before this time, though, when I had finished my university course and had gone teaching at Wangaratta, I borrowed little SD 344 to take my friend, and later fiancée and wife, from Garfield to Lake Emerald for a picnic. We looked forward to a snug time together. Just as we arrived and parked the car, a bus pulled up beside us. It was the Garfield CWA on their annual outing. I recognised everyone on board as they stepped off, one by one. I hid my face behind the sun-shade. Then we beat a hasty retreat.

That year became a strong bonding year between me and my mother. We were home alone, except that Dad was there also at the weekends. Looking back, I can see that it would have been better for me to have gone off away from home, to do something quite different. But it seemed right for me to be with Mum. Without me, she would have been alone most of the time, although that was to come the following year when I went to Melbourne to begin my Arts course.

My leaving was quite an emotional time. Mum felt it very keenly. I remember saying goodbye as I went off to catch the train to Melbourne. Mum watched me as I walked away down the track and through the gate. No sooner was I out of sight than a large tree fell at the end of the paddock, close to the gate through which I had just passed. Mum, always attuned to see signs, felt this to be a true marker of the end of an age. Her children had come, had grown, and had gone.

As for me, my growing up in Garfield was over.

THE END

www.ingramcontent.com/pod-product-compliance
Lightning Source LLC
Chambersburg PA
CBHW020857020526
44107CB00076B/2007